AQUAPONICS AND HYDROPONICS GARDENING

2 IN 1

Learn How to Grow Organic Vegetables, Fruits and Raising Fishes for Beginners

BY

TOM GORDON

TABLE OF CONTENTS

AQUAPONICS GARDENING vi

Introduction vii

Part I - Getting Down To Basics xi

Chapter One - What Is Aquaponic Gardening And How Does It Work? 1

Chapter Two - The Great Matchup: Aquaponics Vs Hydroponics Gardening 5

Chapter Three - What Are The Benefits Of Aquaponic Gardening? 11

Part II - Roll Up Your Sleeves, Let's Get Down To Basics .. 17

Chapter Four - Types Of Aquaponic Systems 18

Chapter Five - Setting Up Your Aquaponic Garden 29

Chapter Six - Setting Up Your Tech-Savvy Aquaponic Garden 41

Chapter Seven - Setting Up A Towering Aquaponic Garden 51

Chapter Eight - Setting Up The Easiest Aquaponic Garden 60

Chapter Nine - What's In Your Water? 66

(More Than You Ever Wanted To Know About Ph) 66

Part III - Filling Your Aquaponic System With Life 76

Chapter Ten - What's On The Menu? 77

Chapter Eleven - For A Small System, Grow A Lettuce Bowl 88

Chapter Twelve - For A Large System, Grow A Vegetable Plate 95

Chapter Thirteen - How Do I Start Growing Plants?........ 105

Chapter Fourteen - Maintenance And Pest Prevention..... 111

Chapter Fifteen - Commercial Applications Of Aquaponic Gardening.. 118

Chapter Sixteen - Make Great Food 129

Part IV - The Science Behind Aquaponic Gardening 145

Chapter Seventeen - Glossary Of Terms.............................. 146

Final Words... 171

HYDROPONICS 176

Introduction 179

Chapter One - Different Types Of Hydroponic Gardens.... 185

Chapter Two - How To Build Your Own System................. 204

Chapter Three - Operation Cycle.. 217

Chapter Four - Best Plants For Hydroponic Gardening And Nutrition... 242

Chapter Five - Maintenance Of Your Hydroponic Garden. 264

Chapter Six - Pest Control 290

Chapter Seven - Myths And Mistakes To Avoid 315

Final Words.. 327

© Copyright 2019 - All rights reserved.

The content contained within this book may not be reproduced, duplicated or transmitted without direct written permission from the author or the publisher.

Under no circumstances will any blame or legal responsibility be held against the publisher, or author, for any damages, reparation, or monetary loss due to the information contained within this book. Either directly or indirectly.

Legal Notice:
This book is copyright protected. This book is only for personal use. You cannot amend, distribute, sell, use, quote or paraphrase any part, or the content within this book, without the consent of the author or publisher.

Disclaimer Notice:

Please note the information contained within this document is for educational and entertainment purposes only. All effort has been executed to present accurate, up to date, and reliable, complete information. No warranties of any kind are declared or implied. Readers acknowledge that the author is not engaging in the rendering of legal, financial, medical or professional advice. The content within this book has been derived from various sources. Please consult a licensed professional before attempting any techniques outlined in this book.

By reading this document, the reader agrees that under

no circumstances is the author responsible for any losses, direct or indirect, which are incurred as a result of the use of information contained within this document, including, but not limited to, — errors, omissions, or inaccuracies.

AQUAPONICS GARDENING

A Beginner's Guide to Building Your Own
Aquaponic Garden

By Tom Gordon

INTRODUCTION

If you like to grow your food, you probably love the feel of soil and revel in the joy of harvesting your crops. Gardens give us pleasure. Gardens date back to our earliest ancestors finding edibles in the wild and learning how to transplant them into a plot of ground. The hanging gardens of Babylon testify to the sense of wonder a garden brings.

What's more, gardening offers other benefits, such as stress reduction, exercise, and stockpiling all that valuable Vitamin D obtained from sunshine. (Vitamin D deficiencies are linked to an increase of heart attacks, type 1 diabetes, and osteoporosis.) Another obvious benefit is the savings factor. In the summer, we eat out of the garden and reduce our grocery bills. I preserve extra for winter use as well. In fact, I cannot imagine life without a garden. However, gardening is not always easy.

Harsh climatic conditions, such as winter weather with a short summer, or life in a desert area, often makes growing your own food a challenge. Plus, watering a garden gets expensive. Maintaining the soil quality can get complicated, buying fertilizer and worrying about keeping it ready for the next season of growth. The good news is, none of that is necessary.

The world of aquaponic gardening beckons you to a new way of cultivating and harvesting your own food, and it's not as hard as it sounds. I know. When I first started researching aquaponic gardening, I was

AQUAPONICS GARDENING

overwhelmed in less than an hour. I have to what? Doesn't it smell? Fish! Ugh! *I don't think so!*

Slowly that distaste grew to grudging respect. The more I learned, the more I wanted to know. After combing countless books and articles, I finally felt ready to embark on this new adventure, but my table lay piled with articles and heaps of paper mocking every attempt at instilling order. When I needed to refresh my memory, I had to rifle through the mess and it was unwieldy at best, a disaster more often than I cared to admit.

Putting all of that information into a format at my fingertips became the genesis of this book. By the time I put it all together, my own floating gardens were a testament to the return of the wonders of Babylon—in my eyes, at least. My neighbors loved the vegetables I was able to share with them, so their praise was hearty as well.

You too can grow your own water-based garden, and it's not as hard as you think. A big plus was my first hand experience in proving it was not stinky after all! I wouldn't have guessed it, but it's true. A properly managed aquaponic garden produces less smell than an aquarium, because the ammonium levels are consistently maintained at the proper level, as opposed to a fish tank no one wants to clean on Monday, Tuesday, or any other day of the week.

To make it easier for friends and family (and that includes you, gentle reader, for you are a new friend), I'm sharing what I've learned. I want to provide you with a more readable, yet complete guide, for following in my footsteps. I'm expecting that some of you have never gardened before, so I'm offering you basic instructions, plus an indexed glossary for added detail. Perhaps you live in an urban area and have never had the opportunity to garden; you'll find aquaponic gardening is perfect for rooftops. Perhaps you live in a climate that doesn't support the required growing season for tomatoes; indoor aquaponic gardening is perfect for you. Don't be afraid to hop on the bandwagon and take advantage of this new option that is igniting the gardening community. I want to give you all the information you need:

- You need to know what aquaponic gardening is and is not.

- You need some convincing before you jump into the water, and so does your family!

- You need to learn about the systems available, and how to choose the best system for your home and garden.

- You need to learn how to set it up, how to maintain it, and how it works.

- Most of all, you need a textbook with a dictionary to learn a lot of new terms and the scientific background to share with disbelieving family and friends. To that end, I have highlighted in bold the terms defined and expounded upon in the glossary at the end of the book. I promise I won't overload you with too much information too quickly, exploding your head and causing you to cast the book aside in despair. Don't worry, we're in this together.

This is your go-to book for creating your own aquaponic garden, a garden you can use year-round, indoors or out, always growing your lettuce bowl or vegetable plate. That's right. With your aquaponic garden, your dinner makins are just steps away. Are you ready to dig in? Let's do this together!

PART I

GETTING DOWN TO BASICS

CHAPTER ONE

WHAT IS AQUAPONIC GARDENING AND HOW DOES IT WORK?

If you're a gardener, you've experienced the joy of planting and harvesting food for the table. Me? I love the beginning and the end...but not so much the middle. You know what I mean: endless weed pulling, regular watering and fertilizing, pest control and manicuring the garden. What if I told you there was a way to bypass that middle step? That would be great, right?

Aquaponic gardening is water-based, not soil-based. It incorporates a built-in source of fertilizing. It's a perfect world where weeding *never happens*. Your garden is a delight for the eyes, and you do it all with little daily effort.

But here's the trick: are you familiar with **symbiosis**? You're going to create a symbiotic relationship between plant and animal. First, you'll set up a water tank with some kind of fish (and we'll get to that), but there are soooo many types of fish, depending on what you want to grow and the size available. Then, you'll create a nutrient-laden water supply (**nutrient film**) and a means for distributing it. Then, you'll plant your seedlings in containers that receive constant water...

The end result? The fish provide the fertilizer. The plants keep the water clean, and you enjoy the harvest. The way you create that optimal brew and the way you distribute it can be derived from several different forms of aquaponic gardening, but the concept holds true for everyone.

A key factor is its **sustainability**. An aquaponic garden is meant to function on its own with a minimal amount of effort. It takes a little information and some work to set it up, a little time to create that lovely nutrient-laden water, but it's all part of the joy in building your very own masterpiece of fish and produce, meshed together in a mutually beneficial ecosystem.

Yes, it's that simple. I expected it to be a daunting procedure. I mean, at first glance, I thought it sounded fishy (bad pun), but the more I researched and put into practice the tips I was learning, the easier it got. The information overload at the beginning left my head spinning, but as I began to take notes, I realized that some people just love to make things difficult. Aquaponic gardening was meant to be *simple*.

- As we progress I hope you're looking up our keywords in the glossary. That's where you'll find all the extra information on each term. Think of this book as a sort of *Aquaponics for Dummies*, with an encyclopedia available as you're ready for more information. I'm including links to help you every step of the way!

You exercise all power in the process. You decide on the system that fits your budget and where you'll put it. You decide on the kind of fish to stock in your water. I began with goldfish, an endless source of delight for children, with a ready supply of salad greens, grown just off the kitchen. You decide whether to grow vertically or horizontally. You decide what to grow.

Best of all, you decide whether this is a hobby, a way to supplement your cupboards, or a way to supplement your income. A healthy market for microgreens is a gateway from experimenting, to then expanding, and then marketing your produce to local restaurants. Winter vegetables straight from the garden to the table are within your reach. Begin small, grow as you are ready.

AQUAPONICS GARDENING

Chapter Summary

- Aquaponics is growing fish to nourish vegetables, and growing vegetables to clean the water for the fish. This is a mutually beneficial arrangement.

- Aquaponics is **sustainable**, a *green* way to live in harmony with mother nature.

- Aquaponics is adaptable for every living situation, from growing a lettuce bowl in your apartment to a commercial enterprise replacing your day job.

In the next chapter, you will learn the differences between hydroponics and aquaponics. By being well versed, you can embark on your project with full confidence in your plan.

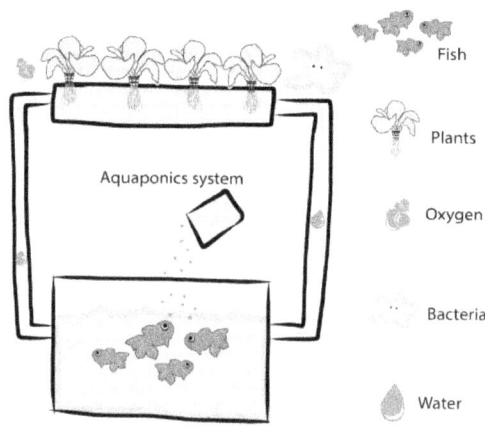

CHAPTER TWO

THE GREAT MATCHUP:

AQUAPONICS VS HYDROPONICS GARDENING

They sound a lot alike, don't they? **Hydroponics** and Aquaponics? They are similar in one way, but vastly different where it counts. Hydroponics means, literally, grown in water. If you take the words aquaculture + hydroponics and put them together, you get aquaponics. Let's look at the two processes in more detail to see why one will be better for you over another.

Ditch the soil. Both systems offer growing a garden without soil. This represents a huge benefit. Soil becomes stagnant after years of cultivation, requiring a lot of fertilizer and/or rotation of crops. Simply replacing the soil during repetitive seasons of indoor growth becomes expensive On top of that, soil is easily contaminated with spores or pests laying eggs, perpetuating all of the diseases from one season to the next. Growing in soil almost requires an outdoor garden, and living in a climate zone with harsh winters means you can only grow your veggies half of the year. Both systems offer value in growing without soil.

Instead of soil, you'll grow your plants in a biosystem of specially cultured beneficial bacteria, and your very own circle of life will sustain both fish and plants. This healthy substitute for dirt is simple to produce, and you'll wonder why you never tried aquaponic gardening before.

Fertilize the water. Both systems require nutrient-based water for plant growth. Hydroponic gardening employs chemical nutrients, which represents constant overhead. You may obtain your growing medium from any number of suppliers, but let's face it: the uncertain role of chemicals in cancer and birth defects is generating headlines around the world. In aquaponics, you may grow *organic* vegetables through natural fertilizer produced by fish swimming around the tank. *The advantage goes to aquaponics.*

Design the right space. Both systems require light and a floor strong enough to withstand some pretty hefty weight. I was clueless. I imagined a sweet little aquarium with plants above it, and was shocked to realize a twenty gallon aquarium weighs a whopping 225 pounds. A concrete floor in the basement sounded smart, but I was hooked on the idea of cute goldfish and had a 14-ft bay window in the dining room, so the scales became my enemy.

- Figure about one inch of fish per gallon of water. If I have a fifty gallon tank, you'll need fifty one-inch goldfish. As they grow, that number decreases.

My research suggested that I needed at least a fifty gallon tank, so I had to adjust my weight limits to six hundred pounds. If space and weight are an issue for you, *hydroponics has the advantage in this case.*

Both systems are going to affect your utility bills. The difference between them is that in hydroponics, the water may not be recycled. In aquaponics, the water must be recycled to formulate the rich growth medium to fertilize the plants. A high water bill would make it cheaper to buy the produce at the market, which makes *aquaponics preferable.*

Both require a growth medium that serves as an anchor for the plants, helps regulate temperature, and provides constant nourishment. In aquaponics, **hydroton** is a popular form made from clay, but see Chapter Four to read more on that subject. I wanted to get a product I was accustomed to using, but all of them were on the no-no list: sand, vermiculite, peat moss, wood chips, and pearlite. On the plus side, this represented a one-time purchase, and I could live with that. I see no strong value of one system over the other, because both require a mix to hold the plant.

Both systems require an investment in setting up the apparatus. A hydroponic garden is cheaper to start if you employ a **wicking** or water culture system. Both require a more complex design for some setups, and hydroponics equals the cost of aquaponics when you add a sump pump and additional piping. Aquaponics requires an investment in fish, but the cost will be less than continually buying chemical fertilizers for the water. In this case, *the plus goes to aquaponics*.

However, the learning curve is definitely higher for aquaponic gardening. Because you are dealing with live organisms to create the fertilizer for your plants, it takes time and experimentation to get the right mix for ideal growth. If you require instant gratification, go with hydroponics. If you like a challenge, like to putter with details, and are willing to wait for results, go with aquaponics. For ease and learning *the plus goes to hydroponics*.

AQUAPONICS GARDENING

Chapter Summary

If you've been keeping score, you already know why aquaponics is favored over hydroponics with homesteaders and survivalists, as well as a growing number of hobby gardeners.

- Aquaponics is cheaper than hydroponics since it recycles water usage.

- Aquaponics is cheaper than hydroponics since a one time investment of fish fertilizes the plants for years, versus buying a constant supply of chemical fertilizers.

- Hydroponics is easier to learn and operate than aquaponics.

In the next chapter, you will learn why aquaponics is the best thing since sliced bread. Just why are homesteaders and survivalists the world over head over heels in love with aquaponic gardening?

AQUAPONICS GARDENING

CHAPTER THREE

WHAT ARE THE BENEFITS OF AQUAPONIC GARDENING?

We already discussed the obvious benefits of aquaponic over hydroponic growing systems. Perhaps you still aren't convinced it's worth the time and hassle to try it out. Read on!

My number one plus for aquaponic gardening is that it is 100% organic. If you harbor any hopes of profiting from your experiment, grow organically certified vegetables. In the United States, the growth of the organic marketplace has mushroomed to more than $39 billion in reported profits. I found that obtaining a certified organic status was an easy process, and I was able to get the paperwork online.

- Even if you choose not to be registered organic, you can tell buyers your produce is *organically grown*. It's a subtle differentiation, but one that satisfies most consumers.

AQUAPONICS GARDENING

Suppose you don't want to sell any of your produce? Still, it's **organic.** Knowing you and your loved ones are eating food with no hormones, chemicals, pesticides, or **genetically modified organisms** (GMOs), is measured in peace of mind. To many, organic foods offer better flavor and texture. And let's face it, nothing is more organic than home grown fertilizer provided via watering from a fish tank. I obviously am a proponent of organic gardening. Beyond that, I'm all for safe food. Recalls, salmonella scares, and bioterrorism cease to worry me when I produce my own food.

A second benefit of aquaponic gardening is needing less water to grow your food. In a closed system of repurposed water, this is a huge benefit. In normal outdoor summer gardening, I stand and hold a hose about an hour a day. Some of that water gets sucked into the atmosphere, some of it runs off, and all of it costs money. Not only will you save money by not manually watering your plants, but your sustainable aquaponic garden recycles the water in your system. Researchers estimate that aquaponic gardens require 90% less water than their traditional backyard counterparts.

A third benefit is the ability to extend the growing season. I live in a temperate zone with hot summers and icy cold winters. I can extend my lettuce bowl crops with a **high tunnel**, but obviously that's expensive and a lot of work. The plastic needs to be replaced every couple of years. A cheap plastic doesn't filter the ultraviolet rays, so there's a few more dollars when going for quality. I still have to utilize row covers in the very early spring and very late fall. Some winters I lose my crop all together. Hail storms and heavy winds wreak havoc on my system. Moving the winter growing indoors into a sustainable system was huge for me.

A fourth benefit was the versatility of aquaponic gardening. It eliminated all concerns over where and when I chose to garden. I could put together a system in my backyard, basement, or living room dependent on individual circumstances. Even if you live in an area with long winters or desert conditions, you can still have a garden.

A fifth benefit was how easy it was to maintain my vegetable garden. It was waist high, so I experienced no back-breaking weed pulling. As a matter of fact, I no longer had to pull weeds at all.

A sixth benefit was being able to streamline my efforts. Like you, my life was and remains a perfect storm of activity at times. Being able to institute a system four to six times more productive per square foot was a huge consideration. I could densely plant my seedlings much closer together, being able to plant twice as many seedlings in the same space as before. Add to that the fact that harvest times came sooner, since the plants grew faster with consistent watering and fertilizing. I liked working smarter, not harder.

A seventh benefit was the opportunity to grow my enterprise. Aquaponic gardening is scalable, meaning you can start with a ten gallon aquarium of goldfish and you can expand your size at will. Utilize the same mechanics and enlarge or reduce your enterprise based on your own schedule and gardening needs.

And last but certainly not least, an eighth benefit of aquaponic gardening rested in the potential of being able to eat my source of fertilizer. True, I was immediately enamored by the idea of growing goldfish, but I soon saw the wisdom in upgrading to a system growing tilapia. Yum! Aquaculture took on a whole new meaning when I was able to grow two crops with one expenditure of effort.

In retrospect, I found so many reasons to embark on this quest to learn and implement aquaponics. If you agree, it's time to get down to specifics.

Chapter Summary

Looking for the benefits of aquaponic gardening?

- Organic gardening at its finest
- Lower water consumption
- Longer growing seasons
- Lower water bills
- Widespread application
- Less work
- Increased productivity
- Scalable enterprise
- More fish dinners

In the next chapter you will learn the basic types of aquaponic gardening systems.

AQUAPONICS GARDENING

AQUAPONIC

Nitrate is absorbed by the plants

Bacteria turns ammonia into nitrate

Water is returned with ammonia removed

Ammonia from fish

PART II

ROLL UP YOUR SLEEVES, LET'S GET DOWN TO BASICS

CHAPTER FOUR

TYPES OF AQUAPONIC SYSTEMS

While this is the most intensive system of growing and providing food on the planet, it does require some special knowledge. You will be meshing a hydroponic (water-based) system with an aquaculture (animal-based) system, and must choose the design that will best meet your needs. You need to know the living requirements of three different kinds of organisms: plants, fish, and bacteria. Finally, you need to build and wire a system that regulates the water for optimal growth factors. That may sound like a lot, but don't be frightened. We'll go through these issues one by one.

The popularity of aquaponic gardening is on the rise, and as you go through this chapter, look for online communities and support groups who can offer you additional firsthand experience for your location. You are entering a worldwide phenomenon and there is no need to reinvent the wheel. You may be able to visit several gardens; comparing and contrasting the features you like.

AQUAPONICS GARDENING

If you are wanting to take a stab at aquaponic gardening, your first decision must be choosing the type of system you want to use. The simplest experiment would be using a sun pond where plants float on the surface with submerged roots. Of course, most of us don't have ponds and are immediately looking at a more sophisticated setup.

Every aquaponic system must include five basic elements:

- a fish tank
- a plant bed
- a means of handling solid waste
- a **biofilter**
- pumps for circulating and aerating water

And these are only the most basic requirements. If you're like me, you'll want a few more bells and whistles, because what's the point of putting in all the effort, only to be met with failure because you decided to go bare bones? For starters, let's look at the types of gardens and then return to these five topics with a little more basic information under our belts.

First, look at space limitations, cost, and ease of maintenance. To help you narrow down your choices, I am describing the options by three classifications: growing a lettuce bowl, growing a vegetable plate, and commercial enterprises. While many a summer found me selling produce at a local farmer's market, I wasn't convinced I wanted to implement an aquaponic garden on that large of a scale, but I nevertheless wanted to look at all options, as will you.

If you are growing a *lettuce bowl*, a **nutrient film technique** (NFT) is your best option. Don't get bogged down in how to build one just yet, but you need enough details to make an informed decision. This is perfect for small plants with shallow roots. Microgreens, all types of lettuce, strawberries, and herbs fall into this category.

The NFT is great for a DIY kind of enterprise. Basically, you will set up your fish tank with a small sump pump running fish water through a PVC pipe with holes drilled into it, and then insert seedlings into a small net attached to each hole. The net offers your plants structure and keeps them from falling through to the bottom of the fish tank. Your plants will extend their roots toward the nutrient laden water, absorbing nutrients much like a paper towel absorbs moisture on a kitchen countertop. A key element is creating a system with a trickle of consistent water flow, rather than a stagnant pool of dank smelly water. These tubes take the place of those traditional grow trays dominating garden centers every spring.

Your NFT system can be as large or small as you want it, as sophisticated or simple as your budget demands. Large sheets of Styrofoam will work just as well as holes drilled into PVC pipes. We'll cover the actual construction in the next chapter, but you want to factor the basic principles into your choice of set up.

Another simple form of watering a nutrient film is an **ebb and flow** system of flooding the growing bed, then letting it drain back down into the fish tank. Your roots are saturated with the nutrient rich water and exposed to it for a longer period of time, in contrast to the dripping method of percolating your water and feeding small amounts to your produce constantly. It requires proximity several times a day or a timer to regulate consistent watering.

A key feature of a garden fed with a nutrient film is creating a bed of growth medium in which the water is made perfect for both fish and plants. It should run through the growth media on its way up to the plants, and then trickle back down to the fish after the plants have done their magic.

A **deep water culture** (DWC) has been valuable throughout history. Early Aztecs (around 1000 BC) created rafts and grew plants resting on their surfaces, with roots dangling in the water. They circulated their water and waste around the rafts to fertilize their crops. Some Asian cultures used ponds and natural sources of water for growing their food, and also created floating gardens. It worked especially well for growing rice.

AQUAPONICS GARDENING

However, you don't need to live by a pond or lake. You can accomplish the same technique with tanks to hold your water. This is perhaps the simplest and least expensive form of aquaponic gardening. Your plants may rest on the surface of the tank, roots fully submerged into the water. You still have the option of inserting canals and pumping the water through two tanks, but you can certainly start small and increase your level of complexity with experience.

You will obviously still need a fish tank to act as a home for your guests of honor. You may still need a **biofilter** to transform fish waste into nutrients for your plants. You will probably want a filter to remove solid waste or plant material from infiltrating or clogging your system. If you install canals, you will need a pump to force water through your system to ensure the water is being recirculated. As with all fish tanks, you'll need an aerator to maintain a high level of oxygen for your environment.

This is scalable, meaning you can use either an aquarium, a stock tank, or plastic tubs. You only need to maintain the correct proportions of volume, fish, and plants to achieve the desired results. I've split up the requirements in maintaining your enterprise from the mechanics of setting it up so your eyes don't glaze over with an information overload. I promise you: it's not hard and you can do this. For now, just decide on how you want to grow your plants.

AQUAPONICS GARDENING

A **media based system** is the option of choice if you want to grow larger plants like tomatoes, zucchini, and other items for your *vegetable plate*. It will function more like your traditional backyard garden, since plants will grow in small pebbles replacing soil. In an aquaponic media-based garden you will incorporate a five step process:

1. Choose a fish tank. You can repurpose an old bathtub in the basement with grow lights or have an aquarium next to a window, but first and foremost, you need a place for fish. The fish eat food and produce waste.
2. Most aquariums already need small pumps for aerating the water. You will also install a small sump pump to cycle water waste to your plants.
3. Your gardening container, ideally about twelve inches deep, will house the growing medium. You will need to purchase some form of **LECA** (Large Expanded Clay Aggregate), a product akin to **hydroton** pebbles, which will provide a petri dish for culturing bacteria from your fish waste. This is where the magic happens. The bacteria convert fish waste laden with ammonia into fertilizer, a nitrate your plants will use for growth. You are creating a sustainable biofilter and your own mini **nitrogen cycle**.

4. Your plants will absorb the nitrates and, in the process, purify the water.
5. Clean water is siphoned back to the fish.

Your final consideration in designing your setup is deciding on how and where you are going to grow your plants. Is this going to be in the backyard? Of course, your climate and your goals dictate the answer to this question, but it bears an impact on the type of system you're creating. Will it be in a **high tunnel**? Will it be indoors with natural light? Will it rest in the basement with **grow lights**? Will you be growing plants vertically? A towering garden works especially well in apartments with limited space and for the artist who wants to create not just a garden, but a work of art.

These questions all figure into your choice of design, and need to be weighed. I recommend looking at the pictures throughout the book , reading through each of the chapters describing how the systems are built, and then sitting down with a pad and paper. Crystallize your needs and hopes, sketch out a plan.

Even though we own a high tunnel, I opted for indoor construction. In our frigid winters, the high tunnel extends the growing season, but when the first freeze hits, all plants go dormant. Only mature plants can be harvested, and then, only in the afternoon as the plants perk up and shrug off the frost. Installing an aquaponic garden in my high tunnel wouldn't provide the kind of fresh vegetables I wanted.

Since I have a dining room with lots of southern exposure and floor to ceiling windows, I opted for an indoor system without grow lights. I also wanted to keep it simple, so I decided on using hydroton pellets in small plastic pots.

If you harbor any qualms about your lighting situation, you can always find a light intensity meter and test the area you want to use for your garden. After putting a lot of time, effort and some expense into setting up your aquaponic garden, you certainly don't want to find out you chose a dark corner where nothing will grow.

Do you see how to work through the decision making process? Take a moment right now to answer questions as your friend or partner might ask them, and come up with your own idea of where you're headed. It's that step of imagining the garden that precedes the construction and planting of any garden.

AQUAPONICS GARDENING

Chapter Summary

Deciding on the type of aquaponic garden you want to install isn't hard once you look at all of the options.

- A nutrient fed system is perhaps the easiest unit to design and operate with success. It includes options of consistent watering through a drip system or periodic flooding with an ebb and flow system.

- A deep water culture requires more planning and preparation, but can be very economical. Its operation requires developing a feel for the perfect watery stew, creating it by running the water through a media bed, and then letting your vegetable roots dally in the water constantly.

- A media bed requires the largest cost outlay and takes the most space. It closely resembles the gardens you may have grown in your backyard, the soil being replaced with the growth medium. Each vegetable is planted in a bed of pebbles.

In the next few chapters you will learn how to construct your aquaponic garden. I'll give you all of the details required in four types of gardens, and I recommend you read each of the chapters before settling on one idea over another. Once you have a basic idea of what is involved in each type of garden it will be easier to choose one. Let's enter the garden gate!

AQUAPONICS GARDENING

CHAPTER FIVE

SETTING UP YOUR AQUAPONIC GARDEN

If You Love a Great Find

Aquaponics is a DIY paradise, so if you're of that mentality, you're going to love this chapter. If you aren't, don't get horrified. I'll cover all of the many ways you can do this and, rest assured, one will appeal to you and work in your circumstances.

The most basic and easiest way to get started is to buy a kit, but some of you are going to want to cobble together a system from repurposed components, and others are going to design a 5th Avenue kind of apparatus. Any kind of receptacle will work as long as it meets these requirements: It must be strong enough to hold water *and* support the growth medium at the outset. It needs to be made from food grade material, safe for fish and plants and bacteria. You will need to be able to connect it to other parts with easily obtained plumbing supplies from a local hardware store. Also, you may need to use a pond liner if it's not watertight by nature.

Now, your system doesn't have to be expensive from the outset, but it will take time: time to build it, time to stock it, and time to develop the right environment to support growth. What is your time worth? Personally, If you live with a Mr. Handyman who would love to sink his teeth into this project, you'll make a good team.

Begin by choosing your site with care. Then begin to start your system. Decide how many fish you want to have and how many plants you want to grow. Count the cost. Don't forget to add in the tank, beds, media, plumbing, lights, pump and aerator, fish, seeds or seedlings, testing equipment, fish food, power, and water. These are basic elements. Sure, if I irrigate the beds and erect canals, I might be able to get by without a sump pump, but just how diligent am I? See what I mean?

Scenario Number One: The DIY Scrounger

So you're a do-it-yourselfer. I can spot you a mile away, and admire your ingenuity. But let's face it: you're not just any do-it-yourselfer. You like to scrounge for your materials and go your own way. You can save a significant amount of moolah by utilizing what you have or finding what you need at thrift stores and junkyards. You'll invest more of yourself and less of your cash, and your new little world will be your baby. There's nothing wrong with that.

Let's begin with some of your basic considerations and how you might choose to build your system. Seamless tanks will last longer than ones with seams. Acrylic tanks will have less of a tendency to leak and should you, heaven forbid, have to move your setup, they are also less breakable. You may fancy repurposing an old bathtub, or want to achieve a beautiful system showcasing the latest technology.

Look at all of the basic components in the systems you investigate. Some require changing cartridges, and that will be an added item to monitor and keep in supply. Since you're handy, only get a pump you can fix if it breaks down or the motor goes out. You can significantly reduce costs if you can extend its lifespan. If you plan on harvesting fish as well as crops, you'll need tanks for breeding purposes. Draw out your plan and make sure you have every component covered.

You think you're ready to start building, but hold your horses. Think and rethink every detail. What shape is your tank? Many suggest that a round tank provides better water circulation and complain that a square or rectangular tank leave more solid waste that must be cleaned out regularly. If you're the artsy type, remember that all those curves and angles represent dead spaces that will decrease your system's efficiency.

AQUAPONICS GARDENING

As you refine your plans and sketch out your design, you'll need to start your shopping list. This represents your most basic needs for a simple system.

1. Find or purchase your fish tank. This is your bottom tank. Make sure it's large enough for both your water needs, but also sturdy enough to support the plant tank, depending upon your design. Personally, I'm salivating over a new outdoor system for the summer with a clawfoot bathtub, but that may be a larger chunk of change than I'm willing to invest. If you're stashing this in the basement with grow lights, it doesn't have to be decorative. If you're creating a visual masterpiece, you can still scrounge for your tank, but it will cost you a tiny bit more.
2. Order a pH test kit.
3. Find or purchase the growing tank. This needs to rest above your fish tank. You can either use two containers that rest upon one another, or fashion a stand to hold the upper tank. Bear in mind that it can rest directly above your fish tank, or stand next to the fish tank, but gravity being a law of the universe, it needs a resting place *above* the first tank.
4. Order your growing medium. As a newbie, I recommend you spring for either **hydroton** or some other version of **LECA** pebbles for your media bed. In creating you own little universe— a living ecosystem—so many things can go

AQUAPONICS GARDENING

wrong, killing your fish and then your plants. I heartily recommend staying with the tried and true on your first go round.

5. You need to purchase an **aeration pump** for the fish tank. Remember that your fish need oxygen.
6. You need to purchase a small **sump pump** to move your water. I've gone into a lot of detail on this in the glossary, because this is the key to your new ecosystem. If you fail to circulate the water, your grow medium doesn't flourish with bacteria, your ammonia never breaks down, and your plants end up living in an arid wasteland without fertilizer. You need a reliable sump pump.
7. Tubing for circulating the water as it is pumped.
8. Gravel. Expect to purchase 2.5 pounds for each five gallons of water.
9. A drill with three different sizes of bits: ½", ¼", and 3/16".
10. Electrical tape
11. Scissors
12. Screws, nuts and bolts, and washers for connecting some kinds of parts.
13. Fish
14. Styrofoam for a growing platform your plants rest upon. (Rafting is the easiest and simplest system. I'll cover channels in the next section for the DIY Engineer.

15. Grow lights to take the place of Mother Nature's sunlight. You may be thinking you can skimp on this. Don't. **Grow lights** represent one of the three basic components of photosynthesis. Your plants need ample sunlight, whether it's from Mother Nature or her buddy building the aquaponic garden.
16. Plants

When you have your shopping list researched and purchased, you're ready for assembly. I hope you're a word person, because I'm going to describe what you're making. I know a lot of you will be saying, "But I need a picture!" Here's the problem with that mentality. A picture is a great guide for comparing your final setup, and I'll give you some links to look at, but you want to *understand* your system inside and out. That requires digesting words and knowing *why* you put things together in a particular way.

Read my instructions before you get too antsy and look for a picture. Remember, you're investing time and money in this endeavor, and you need to understand how each part of the assembly is supposed to function to be able to troubleshoot for problems. There are several basic options available for all of you scroungers, and I'm going to describe just one or two before I give you links.

AQUAPONICS GARDENING

1. Set up your fish tank. If your tank doesn't stand on the floor, it needs a sturdy base. If you are using a wooden crate, put in a durable pond liner. My dining room floor is wood, so I wanted a carpet and plastic liner underneath. My experience proves that water splashes and, as Murphy's law suggests: "anything that can go wrong will go wrong," cautioning safety.
2. Wash your gravel and line the bottom of the tank.
3. Insert your sump pump with hosing rising above the water level. The amount of hose you need depends on just where your growing bed lives. If it's right above the aquarium you need less. If you're running a system adjacent to the aquarium you need more. Give yourself an ample amount of hose.
4. Fill your tank with the desired level of water.
5. Attach your aerator if it isn't submersible, or add it to the bottom if it is meant to be inside of the tank.
6. Measure your water temperature and pH level. I recommend using a spiral notebook with columns drawn for recording your daily readings. It's helpful at the outset to track your progress. Leave space on the side of each line to note changes you've made so that you can make correlations and draw correct conclusions on how your system is affected by each change.

7. Welcome your fish. Just starting out, expect to have one fish per plant for every 10 gallons of water. As your system becomes more efficient, you can expand and play with these numbers. As my experience proves, you can start small with one system, and then expand to another system for the outdoors, and a third with grow lights in the basement.
8. Place your growing bed above the height of the tank. The simplest structure will be a layer of styrofoam resting on top of the tank. Drill holes to release water back into the fish tank. You may prefer a secondary base with your garden bed sitting beside the aquarium. I think it looks nice and it's easier to feed and deal with the fish when the surface of the aquarium isn't obscured by your plant raft.
9. Figure out how, where, or if you need to install **grow lights**. Don't take chances on this. You may have adequate lighting, but if you don't, you're going to waste a month or more of effort in finding that out, evidenced by failing plant growth. At that point you'll be scratching your head and trying to figure out how to cobble together something that works. My best advice is to plan for it from the outset.
10. Whatever kind of receptacle you're growing your plants within, fill it with the soaked LECA pellets or Hydroton. Allow time for all the pebbles to

settle into the base without floating to the surface. You don't want to clog your pump with pebbles getting sucked into the hose, getting lodged in a delicate mechanism.

11. Decide how you're growing your plants. You can cut holes in the Styrofoam and let the roots dangle straight into the water, but you'll need little grow nets to hold the roots and offer structure. You could also cut holes in plastic pots, resting them in the watery base. Personally, I favor the pots. At the outset I was particularly leery of losing little plants into the aquarium or having pellets slip down through the holes. I come from a long line of dirt farmers, so I wanted a method mimicking the process I have always used.

12. Add your seeds or plants. For your maiden voyage I recommend getting small starts from a nursery. Wash the dirt out of the roots, and plant them.

Now, are you ready for some pictures? Here are a few setups created by survivalists and scroungers and I'll list them in the order of my preference. I think you'll see that with some imagination and by *understanding* the steps above, you can combine elements from each into something uniquely you.

Forget that this picture has no fish. It demonstrates the sytrofoam rafting technique of a small indoor aquaponic setup. I particularly like the gravitational flow of this basement application, complete with a grow light. Notice how this stacking system utilizes less floor space, helpful if you live in a small home or apartment. Look at this stylish model! Antiques offer a certain flair, but I like to grow more vegetables than this...but I love that look! I think you're getting the picture of just how simple and economic aquaponic gardening can be, but what if you want a more sophisticated system?

AQUAPONICS GARDENING

Chapter Summary

Survivalists, preppers, minimalists, and crusty old farmers love to cobble together a system on a dime. So do economically minded housewives and people who love the feeling of a simple system.

- Using repurposed supplies lets you put more money into fish and less into structure.
- If you build it from scratch, you'll know how to maintain or repair parts that later demand your attention.
- The more unexpected your design, the more friends and family will rave over it.

In the next chapter, you will learn what the nerds among us love the most—techie and detailed designs.

CHAPTER SIX

SETTING UP YOUR TECH-SAVVY AQUAPONIC GARDEN

If You Obsess Over Design

Some of you have engineering minds. You dream big, and I don't blame you. I favor a more tailored system myself, because I think it increases efficiency and proves how valuable aquaponic gardening really is. Since this isn't a cheap endeavor, talk it over and see what you can afford, where you can cut costs, and how you might streamline the process.

An engineering mind works with precision. You like facts and figures. You always have a blueprint in place before you begin building anything. Does this sound familiar to you? You're either an engineer or you're married to one, and this chapter is for you. An engineer likes all the nitty gritty details, and that attention to detail is what is going to make your garden a marvel.

AQUAPONICS GARDENING

1. Find or purchase your fish tank. This is your bottom tank. Make sure it's large enough for your water needs, but also sturdy enough to support the plant tank, depending upon your design. If you're stashing this in the basement with grow lights, it doesn't have to be decorative. If you're creating a visual masterpiece, pay for a tank that reflects your personality. You'll pay a little more, but you'll love it.
2. Order a pH test kit.
3. Find or purchase the growing tank. This needs to rest above your fish tank. You can either use two containers which rest upon one another, or fashion a stand to hold the upper tank. All engineers know gravity is a law of the universe, so the grow bed needs a resting place above the first tank.
4. Order your growing medium. As a newbie, I recommend you spring for either **hydroton** or some other version of **LECA** pebbles for your media bed. In creating your own little universe—a living ecosystem—so many things can go wrong, killing your fish and then your plants. I heartily recommend staying with the tried and true on your first go round.
5. You need to purchase an **aeration pump** for the fish tank. Remember that your fish need oxygen.
1. You need to purchase a small **sump pump** to move your water. I've gone into a lot of detail on

AQUAPONICS GARDENING

this in the glossary, because this is the key to your new ecosystem. If you fail to circulate the water, your grow medium doesn't flourish with bacteria, your ammonia never breaks down, and your plants end up living in an arid wasteland without fertilizer. You need a reliable sump pump.

2. Tubing for circulating the water as it is pumped.
3. PVC pipe, the length determined by the project width and height.
4. Gravel. Expect to purchase 2.5 pounds for each five gallons of water.
5. A drill with three different sizes of bits: ½", ¼", and 3/16".
6. Electrical tape
7. Scissors
8. Fish
9. The planting receptacles for growing your vegetables, seeds and/or plants.

Many of the basic supplies remain the same as for the scrounger, but what you do with them is as different as donkeys and zebras. You're going to create a wowser of a system.

The Engineer's DIY Aquaponic Garden

Some of the basic components will remain the same. For those of you who skipped over the scrounger's detailed instructions, knowing right away

AQUAPONICS GARDENING

you wanted a more tech-savvy kind of system, let's get to it.

1. Set up your fish tank. If your tank doesn't stand on the floor, it needs a sturdy base. If you are using a wooden crate, put in a durable pond liner. I recommend plastic over a glass aquarium, simply by virtue of weight. Here's the thing: at some point you're going to say, "I think it needs to be shifted just two inches to the left." A glass aquarium is heavy and prone to breakage when dropped. Trust me on this.
2. Wash your gravel and line the bottom of the tank.
3. Install PVC pipes for carrying your water to the plant bed(s), and drill holes or water to get into it at various levels. Be sure it's long enough to attach to the growing medium, so water gets injected into the LECA pebbles.
4. Insert your sump pump close to the PVC pipe. Some go so far as to run the hose directly into it, but I don't recommend doing so. You want more of a trickle of constantly flowing water than a river coursing through your system. Give your bacteria a healthy climate and don't wash them away. A **wicking system** will not work for an engineering marvel like this.
5. Fill your aquarium with the desired level of water.

AQUAPONICS GARDENING

6. Attach you aerator if it isn't submersible, or add it to the bottom if it is meant to be inside of the tank.
7. Measure your water temperature and pH level. I recommend using a spiral notebook with columns drawn for recording your daily readings. It's helpful at the outset to track your progress. Leave space on the side of each line to note changes you've made so that you can make correlations and draw correct conclusions on how your system is affected by each change. Your analytical mind will marvel over all of these details and how each affects the others. You should be in your glory here.
8. Welcome your fish. Just starting out, expect to have one fish per plant per 10 gallons of water. As your system becomes more efficient, you can expand and play with these numbers.
9. Place your growing bed above the height of the tank. Your first PVC pipe needs to be attached to the growing bed, and you'll need a second pipe returning water to the aquarium. You'll replicate this step if you are installing more than one grow bed.
10. Figure out how, where, or if you need to install **grow lights**. This is an engineer's nirvana. Remember these kinds of light generate heat that will affect water temperature, bacteria

cultivation, and plant growth. Look for an energy-saving model.

11. Whatever kind of receptacle you're growing your plants within, fill it with the soaked LECA pellets or Hydroton. Allow time for all of the pebbles to settle into the base without floating to the surface. You don't want to clog your pump with pebbles getting sucked into the hose and getting lodged in a delicate mechanism. Take your time in this step to evaluate your water and have it ready to welcome your plants. Rushing may result in plants that fail to thrive.

12. Figure out the best housing for your plants. Your goal is getting roots into the nutrient film. There are multiple ways to accomplish this objective, but I favor attaching a 2-3 or 4-way fitting to the ascending pipe, then running lengths of PVC pipe across the top of the tank. Drill holes into the pipes and secure the nets. Use another multi connector to bring the rows of plants to the descending PVC pipe. Now, this is a system every engineering heart will rhapsodize over. It's clean. It looks nice. It's efficient.

13. Add plants obtained from a local nursery or grown from your windowsill. Wash the dirt out of the roots, and set them gently into the nets.

Are you ready for pictures? Here's one of my favorites, a series of channels with lots of space for plants, a streamlined design, and convenience at its core.

Look at the way you can expand your system as you get the hang of the process. This commercial application doesn't have to be so massive. You could accomplish the same thing on a more moderate scale. The key in all of these illustrations is in maximizing your gardening space, while that engineering mind does its thing.

The wonderful thing about aquaponics is its versatility. If you've been the reader who pored over the glossary and kept digging for more information, you want a tech-savvy kind of system. Design what makes you happy.

AQUAPONICS GARDENING

Chapter Summary

Designing and building a tech-savvy kind of aquaponic garden requires some of the same tools and concepts, but it's going to appeal to a certain kind of do it yourself genius.

- If you have the engineering mind, banish the impatient and the artistic from your workshop.
- Be patient. It will take longer than you want, but it's going to be a great system.

In the next chapter, you will learn all about maximizing your growing potential as you reach for the sky. Read on.

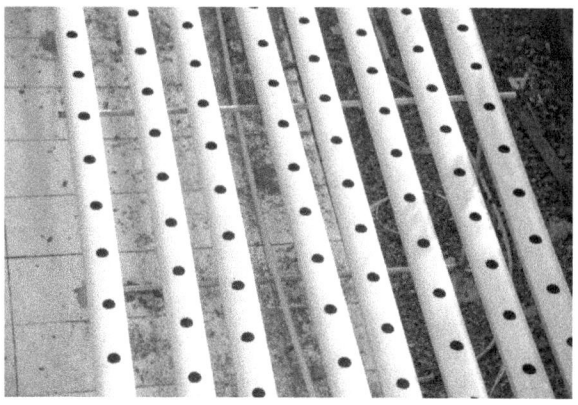

AQUAPONICS GARDENING

AQUAPONICS GARDENING

CHAPTER SEVEN

SETTING UP A TOWERING AQUAPONIC GARDEN

Napoleon's Favorite Option

The idea of growing vertically appeals to me. It takes less space, it's riveting in commanding attention, eliciting a lot of "oohs" and "ahs." It is also more expensive. Don't tune me out. I have my ways, and will help you streamline the process to make it as economical as possible. You may have read the prior two chapters and just not fallen in love with any of the systems outlined. I'm including full instructions here, so you don't have to run back and forth between chapters when you get ready to create your masterpiece. If you're still waiting for the lightning bolt to hit, this may be what you're looking for!

Some of you want the unicorn of all systems, and the tower of gardens is impressive. This will not be a cheap endeavor, and you may still be building it yourself with plans, but what you're creating is more than food for the winter. It's a work of art. It will help if you have construction experience and if you have an engineering mind. Count on learning a lot and *really do your homework ahead of time*.

This system will take time to build, cost more in supplies ,and reap four or five times the amount of produce. Most of the people I know who have creating a towering aquaponic garden, first enjoyed small countertop versions, got their feet wet so to speak, and then built their masterpiece. It is well worth the effort, but this may be your second endeavor, not your first. Your list of supplies will look much like the lists for the scrounger and the engineer with some notable differences. I'm going to describe one way to construct a towering garden, but you'll see pictures and soon realize that there are a dozen ways you can do this.

1. Find or purchase your fish tank. This is your bottom tank. Make sure it's large enough for all of your water needs. Because you're installing multiple growing beds, this is going to take some space, and you'll be ordering more fish to support the additional beds. Depending on how many bedding plants you want, you should probably figure on at least a 100 gallon tank.
2. Order a pH test kit.
3. Order your growing medium. I recommend you spring for either **hydroton** or some other version of **LECA** pebbles for your media bed.

AQUAPONICS GARDENING

Because you're going to transport water to so many growing beds, you need the highest efficiency in your culture. Don't skimp or go cheap in this step.

4. You need to purchase an **aeration pump** for the fish tank. Remember that your fish need oxygen.

5. You need to purchase a **sump pump** to move your water. I've gone into a lot of detail on this in the glossary, because this is the key to your new ecosystem. For a large system, you need one able to move up to 400 gallons of water per hour. This will be your work horse and it needs to be powerful.

6. You need supplies for circulating the water as it is pumped, and in this design, that canal system will function as your bedding containers. You'll spend more on this for towering beds than for either of the other two described projects because you're transporting water further and using it in place of growing containers. I would use PVC piping 3 or 4 inches in diameter. Depending on the number of columns you're designing, you'll need about eight feet per growing column, so do the math and purchase accordingly.

7. Get elbows and T connectors, depending on how many vertical stands you're constructing. I'd plan on four to six. If you're gonna be a bear,

be a grizzly. Build a deluxe system that will meet your growing needs.

8. Purchase hoses or tubes for pumping water to the top of each of the vertical towers.
9. Gravel. Expect to purchase 2.5 pounds for every five gallons of water.
10. Saw horses or a workbench.
11. A hack saw, gloves, and safety glasses for cutting the PVC pipes. You'll probably need sandpaper to smooth those cuts.
12. A heat gun or small torch.
13. A spoon or dowel for fashioning your planting holes.
14. A bucket, cold water, and some rags for cooling the plastic once it's hot.
15. You'll need silicone sealant for attaching those end caps without leakage.
16. An adjustable wrench and two adjustable clamps.
17. A drill with different sizes of bits: ½", ⅞".
18. Fish
19. Plants

I'm not gonna lie. A vertical system is more challenging. Many deluxe kits offer growing towers, especially for hydroponic gardening. If you build one, you'll need to engineer the placement of pipes from a fish tank and then upward to each bed, as well as back down for recycling your water. Why would you go to all this extra trouble and expense? For one thing, you can stack up more growing beds in the same square area with corresponding yields of produce. You will harvest continually, as you can always have a bed of seedlings, a bed of half mature produce, and a bed of veggies ready to pick and put on the table. A towering system is easy on your back with less bending over. It's an easier system to design, since your tubes are traveling up and then down, usually in a straight line. When you construct your first bed, you'll just replicate those steps for each of the beds in your blueprint. Lastly, this is a very flexible system and great for urban settings.

Look at some of these beauties! This system of tiered bins is functional and still pleasing to the eyes. This combines the practicality of the scrounger with the heart of the Napoleonic for a very pleasing combination of towering practicality within anyone's budget. This version incorporates warm wood tones for a craftsman's tower of vegetables.

Let's look at the steps involved in constructing *your* work of art. Because this system utilizes PVC pipe for your growing beds, it is clean and tailored, less messy, and easier to manage.

1. Set up your fish tank with a sturdy base. My suggestion is that it stand below window height, both to discourage the growth of algae and to allow as much space as possible for your towering garden.

AQUAPONICS GARDENING

2. Wash gravel and put it into place.
3. Add the sump pump, and attach an aerator to either the outside of the tank or at the bottom if it is submersible.
4. Now you need to construct your tower. You'll be laying it out on the ground to construct it before you lift it vertically, so pick a good spot as close to its future home as possible.
5. Begin by building a frame for the tower, allowing you to attach each growing tube of plants.
6. Cut your vertical piping. The height will be determined by how tall you want it, and you'll be cutting one length for each tower you want in your garden.
7. You'll need to drill and fashion growing receptacles in each of the vertical pipes. One way is to cut a slit into the pipe, heat with a torch, and then press the soft plastic downward into a lip that will hold your plant. Remember, you can plant all the way around your tube, so dream big and make a lot of plant openings.
8. Drill multiple holes into the end caps and attach them to the base of each grow tube. These allow for drainage back into your fish tank, and you don't want a small pond to develop at the base of the tube, so drill multiple holes.
9. You'll need a horizontal base at the bottom, just above the fish tank for attaching your vertical pipes. You'll also need an identical base at the

AQUAPONICS GARDENING

top to anchor your pipes in another place. Use stainless steel screws, nuts and bolts to prevent corrosion.

10. Fill each pipe with your growing medium. Be sure it doesn't spill out of your pipe lips and into the fish tank.
11. Run water supply tubing or hosing, one for each growing pipe, up your structure. Work the end of each hose into the top of each of the PVC pipes filled with growth medium. It will trickle down and back into your fish tank at the bottom.
12. Add your fish and let your water world do its magic. Keep track of your readings, and when everything is stable, add your plants.

AQUAPONICS GARDENING

Chapter Summary

Designing and building a tower garden combines all the ingenuity of a scrounger, all the tech savvy creativity of an engineer, and all of the imagination of an artist. It is a blend especially for those with less space, who can build upward more easily than outward. These designs are eye catchers and show stoppers, so they are well worth the effort.

- Begin by looking at a lot of pictures to stimulate your imagination.
- Read and understand the instructions above. Many of the principles remain the same in every tower garden.
- Get ready to be the envy of your friends and neighbors. Your garden will be epic.

In the next chapter, you will learn how to be humble. Buy a kit. Take time for a siesta and get some help. It's okay. As a matter of fact, it's a great idea for beginners.

AQUAPONICS GARDENING

CHAPTER EIGHT

SETTING UP THE EASIEST AQUAPONIC GARDEN

If You Want a Kit, For Goodness Sake, Get One!

Some of you looked at the last three chapters and your eyes glazed over. There's no shame in admitting it. You just like to learn by doing, and you feel more comfortable starting with a kit for guaranteed success. I felt much the same way when I started out.

Kits are a great way to break into this world, where one little mishap can kill your fish and sets off a chain reaction, killing your plants as well. There's nothing easier than reading the book and then enlisting the best minds on the planet to create your system for you. In this age of specialization, it's a smart way to dip your toe into the exacting world of aquaponic gardening.

Let's begin by getting some perspective on what's out there. Let's say money is no object. If you've got the space and the money, this deluxe model is like the cadillac of all kits. Let's look at something a bit more modest: This is smaller, but I like its streamlined design and ease of maintenance. Kits vary from the small, to the countertop, to the grandiose, and you get to choose depending on what your budget and your circumstances dictate.

Now, it's time to get down to shopping. Seriously. What should you look for when perusing the internet for kits? Size, for one thing. Will it fit into your space and will it grow the volume of vegetables you're wanting? Nothing is worse than buyer's remorse, spending big bucks on a kit and then realizing it's just not what you wanted. The old theory of spending as long researching as it took you to earn that price tag is particularly sage advice here.

Look at one of the detailed sets of DIY tools and be sure to compare it to other kits as you narrow down your options. Is the kit of your choice complete? Some are less in price, but you have to buy all of the extras, which add up. And heaven help us if you get to a certain stage in the process and then realize you don't have some indispensable part and it will be a week before you get it. Frustration is a killer. One more time. Do your homework.

Think about how easy it will be to clean and maintain the kit. I shake my head at some designs, thinking I'd almost prefer pitching it to cleaning it. Was it designed for a one and done kind of garden? That's not what I have in mind.

Don't forget to check on its safety, using food-grade materials. Some cheap kits don't belong in your home, and the chemicals leached from them don't belong in our bodies.

Look for dealers with experience in building several models. Those models all represent time in the field, and time equals experience. If you have your heart set on a small company with one aquaponic gardening kit, look at it critically and read the reviews.

One small end company is Aquasprouts, with a lot of instruction and supplies for you to begin your search for just the right option. It has earned good reviews, is economical, and a great beginner's garden. It's just too small for my family.

At the other end of the spectrum is the Brio company with two options to consider. It's going to cost you some money. You're going to feel like it's a lot of money, but hold onto your hat. In the world of kits, it's not the most expensive out there.

My favorite is a scalable kit that allows you to choose the size you need. This company carries indoor and outdoor systems, with several models to study. Each of those models translates into time and experience. This company has had time to work out the wrinkles and offers a solid product. This is even more expensive than the gorgeous Brio model, but you get a whole lot more growing power for your money.

Let's say money is no object. If you've got the space and the money, this deluxe model is like the cadillac of all kits. Let's look at something a bit more modest: this is smaller, but I like its streamlined design and ease of maintenance. Kits vary from the small, to the countertop, to the grandiose, and you get to choose what your budget and your circumstances dictate.

My personal fave: I love Murray Hallam's Indy 11.5 system as a cross between a kit and a DIY system, providing the best of both worlds. It is expertly designed and includes 60 pages of full color instructions. You do have to buy the building supplies, but the homework has been done for you. The design is eight years old, and it's a proven commodity. In fact, I'm thinking it may be my next outdoor venture.

What I love most about the kit concept is the way it helps the procrastinator in all of us. Yes, we want an aquaponic garden. Um, yes, we want it with all the bells and whistles. Right now is not a good time, there's too much going on to dig in and design one. Wait! A kit? I can do this over a weekend? Hell, yeah! See how much easier it is to make it happen? This is the answer for all of you wannabes who never seem able to make it happen...life just gets in the way. This is for you!

AQUAPONICS GARDENING

Chapter Summary

A kit is valuable when you don't want to reinvent the wheel. You enjoy building on the brains and tips of pioneers in the field, and end up with a highly-prized aquaponic garden in the process. A kit is valuable when:

- You carefully research the marketplace for the design that is best for your situation.
- You are good at following directions, but lack in personal experience or imagination.
- You like convenience and don't mind paying for it.

In the next chapter, you will learn how to take your aquarium and create the right environment for growing healthy fish. It's all about creating a delicate balance between two toxic extremes.

CHAPTER NINE

WHAT'S IN YOUR WATER?

(MORE THAN YOU EVER WANTED TO KNOW ABOUT PH)

You're about to enter into the most critical phase of aquaponic gardening: adjusting your water so that it welcomes fish and produces the perfect stew for plant growth. We've already covered the basics in the cycle of aquaponic life: fish produce waste. The waste clings to inorganic matter (clay pebbles), where colonies of bacteria break down the waste into nitrates the plants can digest. The plants absorb the nutrient laden stew and return it to the fish as clean, wholesome water.

I know that sounds easy, but the truth of the matter is that it's not. You need to create just the right watery stew for optimal fish growth that becomes the right watery stew for plant growth. That involves the level of oxygen, the temperature of the water, and the right degree of acidity. Of these three, acidity is the key factor.

Strap on your seatbelt, because you're about to learn more than you ever wanted to know about **pH balance**. I'm going to offer you a primer in this chapter, and a lot more information in the glossary, complete with links in case you want to delve into the subject further.

First, the basic definition and its explanation. In all of life, there exists a delicate balance of positivity and negativity. Just as in the building blocks of nature, elements present within a sphere of a positive nucleus, jam packed with protons and neutrons and orbiting negative electrons. They are happiest when perfectly balanced in a neutral state. In a chemical reaction, the electrons shift. Think of a parking lot with cars parked in all of the parking stalls. A whistle blows, and every driver races around the lot to park his car in a different stall. In the process, these elements exchange electrons, each attracting or losing electrons, collecting different configurations, and thus creating compounds. Hydrogen and oxygen become gaseous or liquid water, its chemical composition being two parts hydrogen and one part oxygen (H_2O).

Their combination into water creates a stable substance with a perfect balance between positivity and negativity. If you possessed super powers and could look down to see what is happening at the most basic level, you'd see a chemical reaction in which hydrogen was stripped of its electron, making it positively charged. Oxygen was stripped of two electrons, making it negatively charged. They combine in such a way that the extra electrons in the two hydrogen atoms join the vacant parking stalls in the oxygen atom, and suddenly, both have reached a perfect state of neutrality.

This replay of trading electrons and forming new substances goes on all day long in your body in the millions of exchanges regulating the transmission of thought at each synapse, as well as the charging and recharging of each heartbeat. It happens automatically without any effort on your part, and until right now, you may not have even been cognisant of the miracle of life taking place inside of you.

The study of this perfect body stew is called **homeostasis**. That's a fancy word that means keeping the body primed at just the right amount of acidity so these millions of chemical reactions take place. Your body likes a pH of 7.35 to 7.45. Your arterial blood is normal at 7.40. That's a very narrow range for supporting life, but your body maintains it through the transfer of electrically charged elements of calcium, sodium, carbon, and potassium, to name a few.

The measure of acidity or alkalinity is done through measuring the pH. It ranges in a scale from 1 to

14. A lower pH means that your measured substance is more acidic. A higher pH means that your measured substance is more alkaline. Let's look at that water molecule we created at the beginning of the chapter. When water rains down upon us, it is neutrally charged at 7.0. When chemicals get dissolved into the water, its balance shifts.

Acidic substances donate electrons to become negatively charged, and in the process, combine with positively charged substances to create another neutral compound. Everything you see taking place around you depends upon these teeny tiny chemical reactions, moving and parking electrons, changing parking stalls, and always looking for just the right place to land.

When you read the next chapter, you'll be analyzing what kind of watery stew each fish likes. Some live within a very narrow sphere, like your body, and some tolerate wide fluctuations in the acidity versus alkalinity of their watery home. It's going to be your job to create that delicate pH balance your fish like, so just how do you do that?

Your first step will be measuring your aquarium pH. You'll use a kit with litmus paper strips. Dip one into the water and see it turn a color representing its place in the scale of measured acidity or alkalinity printed on the side of the jar containing the litmus strips. It won't matter if you're color blind, because you'll still see some hue in the scale and still be comparing your strip to whatever that color looks like to you.

Most fish will tolerate the water you put into the tank. However, that water won't stay at the neutral pH after the fish begin to inhabit their new home. As they expel waste, they add ammonia (NH_3) into the water. This is a charged compound, making the water acidic. If that waste builds up, you'll begin to smell ammonia, and if it continues to increase, it will reach a toxic level for your fish, preventing the flow of oxygen into their gills, effectively asphyxiating or drowning them. In a normal aquarium you'd be changing the water to make it neutral once again.

That's a different kind of exercise when you have a 50, 100, or 500 gallon tank of water. This is where your clay pebbles come into play. They house bacteria that cause important chemical reactions. One type of bacteria (nitrosomonas) will change the NH_3 to NO_2 (a nitrite), and another bacteria (nitrobacter) will take the nitrite and change it into NO_3 (a nitrate). This nitrate is just what your plants need to grow, and they'll absorb it into their roots. You can't effectively add plants until these nitrates are present in the water, and it can take up to thirty days to get a healthy environment up and running.

★ The **nitrogen cycle** is the process of keeping your aquaponic garden running like the rest of the universe, in a constant recycling of nutrients.

Here's the normal progression you'll see when you add your fish to the water. First, you'll record an increase in acidity, as your fish excrete waste into the water. Then, you'll see a shift, as the bacteria kick in and start doing their magic. That's when you may introduce plants, which will cleanse the water as they absorb these nitrates.

In the process of it all, you'll need to measure your water's acidity as well as levels of nitrites and nitrates, every couple of days to be sure the optimal balance is being maintained. If it becomes too acidic, you'll need to exchange water or lessen the waste by feeding your fish less.

Nitrates, however, are just one measurement involved in maintaining a healthy aquaponic garden. Just as important is the regulation of water temperature. Your fish will be cold-blooded. Why does that matter? They cannot generate body heat and it falls upon you to regulate the water to their comfort and health. When a child's temperature rises just three degrees, we become concerned over the fever and work at reducing his/her temperature. Your fish will suffer similarly when you're water temperature fluctuates wildly.

★ Aim for no more than three degrees of change within a given twenty-four hour period.

Factors affecting your tank water temperature include your heat source, your climate, and how warm or cool your keep your home (if indoors), the amount of piping your water travels through, how you place your tanks, your growing bed, and whether or not you insulate parts of your system. Of course, you want to reduce your energy consumption and thereby reduce your cost of operation. For this, one of the simplest things you can do is to insulate your tanks, grow bed, and pipes. All of this requires a willingness to set up your tanks and to monitor your conditions before investing in either fish or plants.

You also need to monitor the oxygenation of your water. We've covered getting an aerator to add oxygen, but how do you know if you have the amount of fish you need? The level of dissolved oxygen directly affects your fish growth, and the level of nitrifying bacteria for converting waste into fertilizer. Your goal is 100% oxygen saturation, and to do that you must mimic Mother Nature. Streams and rivers remain oxygenated by air bubbles trapped in molecules of water during rainfall. They dissolve into the water and increase the oxygen level. In your aquarium, you mimic this process through the use of an **aeration pump**.

All of this discussion points to getting a good kit for measuring your water and for keeping records. **Water testing kits** come in many different forms, some more expensive than others:

1. The handiest and cheapest form are dry test strips. The reagents are already applied and the

color changes pinpoint measured levels, comparing them to the guide on the jar.
2. Liquid test kits require you to take samples of your tank water, add reagents, and then read the color after some time has elapsed. These are very accurate.
3. The most expensive form is a photometer, requiring frequent calibration.

Look at the links in your glossary and find one that meets your needs. Don't be scared by the prices you see when you start shopping for a kit. Yes, they are expensive, but think about how long they last. Each kit has a lot numbers printed on it, and usually the last four digits are the month and year it was manufactured. You'll want to keep track of that number, because your equipment lasts a long time.

AQUAPONICS GARDENING

Chapter Summary

Maintain the proper level of acidity or alkalinity in your water by:

- Measuring your water pH level several times each week.
- Lower the acidity by exchanging water in the tank.
- Lower the acidity by feeding your fish less.
- Lower the acidity by introducing plants.

In the next chapter, you will learn about which fish you want to invite to your new fishy home.

AQUAPONICS GARDENING

PART III

FILLING YOUR AQUAPONIC SYSTEM WITH LIFE

CHAPTER TEN

WHAT'S ON THE MENU?

You already know your fish tank can become a home to everything from ornamental koi to cod, but you have to decide on which fish to purchase. This chapter is devoted to looking at some of your choices and the types of factors that will influence your decision. Among your most basic considerations are cost, how quickly they reproduce, and your growing conditions.

Ornamental Fish—Koi and Goldfish

These lovelies are not edible, but they are certainly good looking.

Koi can live in temperatures ranging from 59 to 77 degrees Fahrenheit, requiring a pH of 7 to 8. They are hardy, easy keepers, and long living. At maximum size, they can grow to two feet over thirty years.

Goldfish come in two varieties, denoted by their tails. The single tail is more aggressive than the double-tailed variety, and breeders don't recommend putting both in the same tank. They love a temperature between 78 and 82 degrees Fahrenheit, pH 6 to 8. They are hardy and can reach a pound in size within one year.

Comet goldfish are American-bred with deeply forked tails. They come in several colors and can grow to twelve inches in length over 10 or 15 years.

Shunbunkin goldfish originate from Japan. They are very attractive and can grow to over 15 inches in length.

The lion head goldfish are very popular, because of their distinctive heads and various colorings. They live up to 15 years, but seldom grow more than 6 inches long. When we look at the number of fish you must carry, keep that smaller size in mind.

Fantail goldfish are extremely hardy and great for beginners. They have a distinctively short, egg-shaped body with a wide head. They may grow up to 10 inches in length over 15 years.

Other ornamentals, such as tetras and guppies are less hardy and more demanding. Also, bear in mind a few caveats. Many ornamentals have been treated with antibiotics or other chemicals that are stored in their flesh. Yes, they are bringing those to your aquaponic garden. Ornamentals have also been known to carry TB, worms, and other parasites.

Tilapia

If you're ready to dive in with fish you'll eventually be eating for dinner, one of the most common is tilapia. Did you know there are three species of tilapia? Neither did I. There are white, gold, and blue tilapia.

The gold tilapia is a tough species, and can tolerate water temperatures anywhere between 75 and 98 degrees Fahrenheit, and need a pH of 6.5 to 9. They can survive poor water quality, pollution, and low levels of oxygenated water. They are also the most disease resistant. The blue tilapia grows much more slowly, taking as long as 3 years to reach 2 to 4 pounds. The white tilapia is an offshoot of the blue species, but it grows as fast as the gold and survives temperatures as low as 50 degrees Fahrenheit.

If you're wanting a faster turnover from fish to vegetables on the table, the white is the better choice. About this point you should be wondering what these fish eat. Off the shores of Hawaii, they would eat algae and tiny one-celled organisms, but you're going to be eliminating algae from your tank. That means you need to buy an organic source of **fish food.** Some cheaper versions will be made from fish waste, crushed bones, and other byproducts, but these are not good for your fish, especially if you plan on harvesting them for table consumption.

★ Feed your fish well, and they can grow to full size in as little as eight months. Feed them poorly, and they may never gain a pound.

Full grown tilapia are a delicious addition to your dinner table. To harvest them, it is recommended that you put them into a separate tank for three to five days, withholding all food, thus cleansing the digestive tract.

How large a tank do you need to grow tilapia? A fully grown fish needs three gallons of water. That equals one fish per every 3 to 6 gallons of water. Let's look at those figures realistically. If you are growing tilapia, you are looking at a tank holding about 130 gallons, able to handle 20 to 40 fully grown tilapia.

To summarize, tilapia are the most popular of the large fish in aquaponic gardens, because of their relatively fast rate of growth, hardiness, and mild flavor. Expect to spend money on organic food and a water heater, and make sure you have a large tank.

Pacu

This fish comes from a region with jungles and rainforests, so it requires warm water (between 75-88 degrees Fahrenheit), pH 6.5 to 7.5. They do not live amicably with other fish, so even though they don't feed off them, refrain from putting them together. Also pay attention to its full grown size: 3½ feet long and 88 pounds. Do I need to warn you about having a very large system?

Catfish

These are actually great fish for your aquaponic garden. They grow to full size within one year and are known for their hardiness when a tank's system gets polluted. In addition, they do well in temperatures between 75 and 86 degrees Fahrenheit, pH 7 to 8.5, making them easy keepers. Catfish grow no scales, so plan on skinning them before they hit the pan.

On the plus side, you can add some variety to your tank, because this is not a territorial species. On the minus side, they need a high protein fish food, so keep that in mind before investing in them. Midway through the year you don't want to suddenly feel like you are spending *way too much* money on fish food and experience buyer's remorse.

Trout

Prized by gourmands, this is a fun breed to grow. They tolerate colder water, so be sure you want to grow vegetables that will also tolerate cooler water, around 45 to 65 degrees Fahrenheit, pH 6.5 to 8. They grow slowly and enjoy an eclectic palate of fish, insects, and small invertebrates. Those all sound attractive until you look at the other side of the coin.

These fish don't play well with other species. Be sure you only want trout. They need a lot of space and they grow slowly. They also require higher levels of oxygenated water (a minimum of 10 mg/min), so plan on getting a high quality aerator for your tank.

Carp

These fish are popular in Asia, but not so much in most Western cultures. As a matter of fact, in the United States, where they are considered pests, you may get fined for having them. Surprisingly, the goldfish is a smaller and distant relative to the carp, a testament to the species' versatility.

Cod

If you don't want to heat your water, the murray cod is an excellent choice, as it withstands a range of 46 to 75 degrees Fahrenheit, pH 7 to 8. It grows to an adult weight of 1 pound in 12 to 18 months. They make great friends for different kinds of perch, but realize they are omnivorous and will eat smaller fish, even resorting to attacking one another if you neglect to feed them enough. These fish enjoy a very long lifespan of up to 15 years, so if you don't plan on harvesting them for the table, they make a great investment in your aquaponic garden.

Jade Perch

A native of Australia, this fish tolerates water temperatures of 60 to 85 degrees Fahrenheit, pH 6.5-8.5. One thing that endears it to aquaponic gardeners is its taste for vegetables and vegetable waste, eating scraps normally composted. It will grow to one pound in twelve months. This is an excellent fish for the table, as it is high in omega-3 fatty acids.

Bass

American fishermen prize bass, and enjoy their mild taste. They tolerate water temperatures of 65 to 80 degrees Fahrenheit, pH 7.2 to 8, and reach maturing in one year. There are several kinds: large-mouth, smallmouth hybrid striped, and white bass. If you catch them from a local pond or lake, you can transplant them into your aquaponic garden, eliminating the cost of buying them.

Barramundi

A native of Asia, plan on keeping water temperature higher for this breed of fish: 71 to 80 degrees Fahrenheit. They eat a lot, so of course there will be a lot of waste, which can put your system out of whack. The adult fish will eat the fingerlings, so don't plan on keeping breeding fish together.

This is a fast-growing fish, but experts suggest it's not the best fish for beginners. Take their advice.

Crappie

This species comes is different sizes and colorings. They take two years to grow to a full size of one 1 pound, so don't expect a fast turnaround. They tolerate water between 60 to 75 degrees Fahrenheit, pH 6.5 to 8.2, making them quite hardy. They will be happier living with their own kind, and so will you.

Blue Gill

Native to North America, these are common in the United States. You will find them easy to catch and transfer to your aquaponic garden. They like their water between 70 and 75 degrees, a narrow range to manage, and like a pH of 7 to 9. It makes many friends in the fish family and will reach table size in one year.

Freshwater Prawns and Shrimp

These are very profitable fish to raise and sell as part of your aquaponic garden, as they are the number one source of seafood consumed worldwide. They tolerate water temperatures between 57 and 84 degrees Fahrenheit, pH 6.5 to 8, and may be harvested within 3 to 6 months. They don't like change, so stabilize your tank before obtaining them.

Salmon

These are delicious fish, but very large, needing very large tanks. They like a temperature of 55 to 65 degrees Fahrenheit, pH 7 to 8. It takes 2 years to grow one to full size. They are tolerant of cool conditions, but realize that you can't manage them out of doors if you live in a temperate climate with hot summers. They are not resistant to disease and require more food per pound than all other fish used in aquaponic gardening.

AQUAPONICS GARDENING

Chapter Summary

In this chapter, we reviewed the many types of fish available for aquaponic gardening. Choice of which fish you want to employ in stocking your tank rests on variables such as size, cost, ability to get along with friends, and life requirements. Choosing to harvest your fish requires setting up a breeding tank to ensure you always have a supply of new fish coming on to replace the ones you harvest. There is a fish for every aquaponic enthusiast:

- ornamental fish
- tilapia
- pacu
- catfish
- trout
- carp
- cod
- Jade perch
- bass
- barramundi
- crappie
- blue gill
- freshwater lobster or shrimp
- salmon

AQUAPONICS GARDENING

In the next chapter, you will learn about the vegetables you may want to grow in your aquaponic garden.

CHAPTER ELEVEN

FOR A SMALL SYSTEM, GROW A LETTUCE BOWL

Because we wanted a small indoor system where we could enjoy the fish and easily harvest our produce, I first opted for growing a medley of veggies great for a lettuce bowl. I cannot remember making salads with just one kind of lettuce, so for me, it's always about the blend of flavors and colors. Adding peppers, tomatoes, cucumbers, chickpeas, hard boiled egg quarters, strips of smoked cheese, nuts, and fruits always takes a back seat to a great bed of greens.

For a home garden, I choose different greens from a commercial perspective—I use larger leaf lettuce over microgreens. When I mix up a huge salad bowl, I'm normally feeding 12 to 16 people. We entertain a lot, so sometimes I'm feeding 25 or 30. For those numbers, I'm more interested in how much salad I'm making rather than whether or not gourmands are impressed with those tiny, highly valued microgreens. So, unless it's just the two of you, or your family picks at salads (so why are you growing greens?) I recommend the following:

I always grow two types of lettuce. The green varieties vary based on my mood when I plant, but my favorites are romaine and black seeded Simpson. In addition, I always grow a ruby lettuce variety. It's tangier, so it adds both color and bite to the salad bowl.

Also, I always grow spinach as one addition to the salad bowl. Harvest the leaves when they are small for a sweet, delicate flavor. Pinch off any tendency to bolt.

★ Freeze the seeds for a day before planting them to hasten the germination process.

Kale is an important staple in our household. I often add it to salads, but I also love to wash the leaves and freeze it. I don't blanch it. I just wash and dry the leaves, stuff them in freezer bags, and toss them into the upright. When I make soups or stews during the winter, I take a bag out, crush up all the leaves and pour them in for extra vitamins, nice color and definition, with a bit of a punch. When it comes to cooking fresh kale, my family prefers to ignore anything healthy. They like for me to fry up a mess of bacon. Then saute in some minced garlic, add the greens, wilt it all, and top it with the bacon. (Don't yell at me. They're eating greens!)

If I grow any microgreens for my table, it's a plant or two of arugula (a little goes a long way) and a few watercress. In Victorian days, watercress sandwiches were quite a delicacy, but in my family, not so much. We like it in salads, and like the crinkly-edged leaves the best.

Pak choi is another vegetable many opt to grow, though it isn't one of my regulars. It is a form of Chinese cabbage and you'll find it in several dishes at Chinese restaurants. You'll find it very suitable for your aquaponic garden because of its compact growth and densely green, nutritious leaves. It can grow in partial shade and in containers, making it a great choice for a lettuce bowl over a vegetable plate.

Herbs earn a prominent place in my indoor garden. Of course, I don't grow all of the following all of the time, but my top choices are Italian parsley, rosemary, and mint. Let me give you a few words about each one.

Italian parsley is a wonderful garnish for spaghetti and lasagna, or any form of pasta. It tastes mild and the color, sprinkled over the top, earn rave reviews before anyone takes that first bite. It never disappoints.

I like to grow basil and use it in soups and stews. I also like to harvest it to make pesto. I put the pesto into small ice cube tray compartments, freeze it, and then put them into little baggies in the freezer. It's easy to extract a small amount of pesto to garnish any dish. I've added an easy, no fuss pesto recipe to a later chapter, in case you're new to it.

Thyme is wonderful on poultry. No turkey gets roasted at our house without two or three handfuls of thyme to season both the meat and the stock. If it matures before Thanksgiving, I simply harvest the plant, tie it up by the kitchen window to let it dry, and break off what I want when it's time to use it.

I use mint in the summer for tea, lemonade, and strawberry salads, but I never want to grow it out of doors. It's a highly invasive plant, so an aquaponic garden is the perfect place to contain its wandering ways.

Chives are wonderful to have on hand with baked potatoes. A baked potato bar is a favorite meal in our household, and everyone loves to sprinkle snipped chives over their sour cream—as well as cheese, bacon, broccoli, and a medley of wonderful toppings.

Sage assumes a huge role in our household. Besides offering a savory twist to stews and dressing mixes, my family loves it crushed into their biscuits for a Saturday morning biscuits and gravy feast.

I only grow a few sprigs of rosemary. I love it on meatloaf, but it's not high on my list of stocked staples.

Last, but not least, cilantro is not easy to grow due to its tendency to bolt, but we eat so much Tex-Mex, I have to grow it. The nice thing about growing your own stash is that when you buy a bunch at the market, it has a short shelf life. You'll be able to harvest just the right amount you need for salsa, guacamole, or as a garnish.

AQUAPONICS GARDENING

Chapter Summary

If you have a small aquaponic garden, growing a salad bowl is a wonderful use for your space. You will enjoy the benefits of lovely fish and the fresh veggies that make salads a memory.

- For a home salad, grow several varieties of lettuce and spinach.
- Kale is valuable in smoothies, cooked as a vegetable, or frozen for winter stews.
- Fresh herbs are wonderful as garnishes and flavorings.

In the next chapter, you will learn about vegetables for a larger aquaponic gardening setup.

AQUAPONICS GARDENING

CHAPTER TWELVE

FOR A LARGE SYSTEM, GROW A VEGETABLE PLATE

You don't have to be a vegetarian to love vegetables, and you don't have to grow a wide variety to be a successful gardener. As a matter of fact, in aquaponic gardening, you are well advised to choose carefully those foods you eat the most, and focus on selectively growing a smaller variety of plants.

Some do especially well in your setting, and among those are tomatoes, peppers, cucumbers, beans, squash, peas, broccoli, cauliflower, cabbage, and peppers. As a matter of fact, depending on the size of your fish tank and the size of your growing bed, some are better suited for indoor growth than for outdoor cultivation. Let's go through them.

Tomatoes

This is a mainstay in our household. In the summer in my outdoor garden, I often grow up to 100 plants, just to be sure I have enough to turn into luscious salsa, tomato juice, tomato sauce, spaghetti sauce, and still have plenty to put on the table. You may find the vast numbers of varieties overwhelming, so let's go through the basics.

Whether you have an indoor or an outdoor system, and whether you have space for one, twenty, or fifty plants, you'll still want to look carefully at all the varieties available. If you plan on growing your plants from seeds, look at two great companies. Burpee seed company has been around long enough to win respect nationwide and you can't go wrong with anything you order from them. I prefer Johnny's for their selection of non-GMO and organic offerings.

If you want to plant them in an outdoor garden, start them right after Christmas. I like to have well-developed roots and strong plants to transplant into the garden. I start in plenty of time, using either trays or plug flats. When the plants have true leaves, I flip them out carefully into a larger receptacle and let time do its magic. I plant them in soil and then wash my roots for transplanting them into an aquaponic system.

I like a nice slicer for table use, and Johnny's Big Beef F1 is a great beefeater for BLTs. Since this one is a hybrid (denoted by the F in its title) variety, you can't save and replant the seeds. It ripens in about seventy days, and is resistant to several diseases. I plant the full packet so that I can share seedlings with friends and sell some to recoup my costs.

We eat a lot of cherry tomatoes, and I order Johnny's Supersweet 100 F1. It is known for being prolific and as a sweet snack—a great combination. We like to pop them in our mouths whenever we work in the garden.

Many grow a special variety for tomato paste, but we use whatever I have and just cook them down until they are nice and thick, If you want a specialty tomato just for paste, try Johnny's Amish Paste variety, which is both organic and heirloom. You can save these seeds from one year to the next.

If I don't get my seeds started, I end up getting small, established plants from a local nursery. I fall head over heels for too many varieties, and go home with a medley of Jet Star, Early Girl, Beefeater, and...well, you can see where this is going. By the end of the summer, my plant tags have washed or blown away and I have no idea which plant is which. I'm just plucking and the family is canning like crazy.

You can see why I favor an indoor aquaponic system, growing just what I need for table use. It is so much more manageable, and I end up with tomatoes year round.

Peppers

AQUAPONICS GARDENING

Peppers are the second villain in my over-burgeoning outdoor garden. I am never content with just a simple bell pepper. Oh no. I have to have two varieties of bell peppers, along with yellow, orange, and red peppers. Then I need several kinds of warm peppers, jalapenos and what not for salsas.

An indoor aquaponic garden usually limits me to one pepper plant, and I pick my favorite. I like Johnny's Gourmet F1 orange bell pepper for salads and for family eating. We slice them into strips to take the place of potato chips, and love their sweet flavor. A close second is their Carmen, an organic F1 corno di Toro Pepper seed. One of our favorite vegetable medleys is green beans sauteed with strips of pepper and craisins. This pairs well in that medley of flavors. (See the recipes in this book!)

Squash

We love zucchini and I like to grow it indoors. Squash bugs destroy plants early in the season, despite multiple efforts to prevent them. We often plant them outdoors after the 4th of July, and the plants survive longer than when planted in the spring, but still fall victim to those sap-sucking borers in the course of time. We relentlessly pick off the pests and feed them to the chickens, but that only delays the process. We maniacally check for eggs deposited underneath the leaves and scrape them off carefully, but we still end up losing our plants, and I hate paying for zucchini at the market when I had it in my garden just a few weeks before hand.

My top choice are the summer squash. You already know I love zucchini, and if you have limited space, one plant can take up three feet as it grows and blossoms. As such, you can probably only have one, so choose wisely.

Cucumbers

I favor an English cuke with an edible skin. I like the long, narrow seedless varieties over the typical fat cucumbers you see in stores. Johnny's Poniente organic F1 is a great choice, as is the Socrates F1. Both are thin-skinned, have excellent flavor, and are disease resistant. Plus, both are great for indoor gardens.

If you grow an upright version and tie up the vines as it grows, it doesn't have to take up a lion's share of your space. I use small trellises so I can spread out its branching growth. I have used garden fencing, but too many cukes ended up growing on the other side of the fence and were hard to pick, so I went back to a more traditional trellis. They make such a lovely sight, dangling there and inviting themselves to lunch.

Beans

An indoor plant is wonderful for table use. I love to pick a few beans and steam them for supper, without having to pick a bushel for canning. Over and over, I think you're seeing the advantage to an aquaponic garden when it comes to growing a vegetable plate. You're looking at quality of produce, not volume.

I still would grow an upright variety of green beans over a bush, just to make it lovely and to save some space, but there are several varieties to choose from. Johnny's Jade is an excellent pole bean with long sweet fruit that presents well in a vegetable plate.

Beans need successive plantings to maintain a consistent harvest, so bear that in mind as you plan out your space. You'll need to start a cycle of plantings, seedlings, transplants and rotate them on a regular basis.

Peas

I admit it. I don't like cooked peas. For me it's a texture thing, because I love to eat them raw in salads and as snacks. Whether you are a pea lover or not, however, peas are great for your garden.

If you are planning a traditional outdoor plot, in addition to your indoor aquaponic garden, peas are your new best friend. The plant can be tilled into your garden to feed it valuable nutrients at the end of the growing season, and you can use your indoor plants to good advantage. My favorite is Johnny's Super Sugar Snap, which is great sauteed with strips of peppers and green beans. They also taste great in salads and in Chinese dishes.

Broccoli

I find broccoli better suited to indoor than outdoor growth, as it often bolts in my garden and proves good for nothing. Johnny's Eastern Magic F1 is my favorite variety. The added benefit of growing it indoors in an aquaponic garden is fewer caterpillars and slugs. You don't have as many hard-to-find pests to remove prior to eating your produce either.

Cauliflower

Have you looked at the price of cauliflower at your local market lately? Because it serves as a low glycemic substitute for potatoes, it has grown in popularity. Growing your own is a great alternative to watching for sales. I'm a bit of a purist, and prefer Johnny's Amazing variety over all of the purple and other unusual types of plants.

Be careful in growing it, as it likes a mild 70 degrees and your fish may find that a little warm. Grow lights add heat and will not be your friend. It is traditionally an early spring or late fall kind of crop, but you can tailor your indoor conditions successfully with a little care.

Cabbage

This is another of my least favorite vegetables in the garden. It is harvested by the head, and deep down inside the plant I find all kinds of worms when I start to clean and separate the leaves. As a result, it is perfect for your aquaponic setting. Just realize that it takes up a fair amount of space and is only good for one harvest.

Chapter Summary

You don't need a huge aquaponic garden to enjoy some of these larger, delectable vegetables all year long. My top pick is the tomato, but you have a lot of options.

- A vegetable plate suggests several kinds of plants. Grow one or two of each.
- Choose those you can grow within your own space confines. You have a lot of choices:
    - Tomatoes
    - Peppers
    - Squash
    - Cucumbers
    - Beans
    - Peas
    - Cauliflower
    - Cabbage

Once you've decided *what* to grow, you have to decide *how to start growing it*. In the next chapter, we'll explore ways to get your garden established.

AQUAPONICS GARDENING

CHAPTER THIRTEEN

HOW DO I START GROWING PLANTS?

By now you're probably rarin to go, but still wondering: "How on earth do I get started?" This is a legitimate question. For those of us who have gardened in the backyard, we know exactly what to do: broadcast some seeds, cover them with soil, keep them moist, and voila! Plants appear.

In an aquaponic garden, things are a little different. I'll go through three ways and leave you to figure out the best option for your situation. Realize there is no one right way.

First of all, you can propagate seedlings as you always have, starting them in potting soil. If you choose this method, pay attention to instructions. Lettuce should be covered with a bare quarter inch of soil. Let your seedlings grow there at least until the second leaves (the true leaves) pop out. Gently lift them from your soil and rinse away any debris that might clog the filters in your tank. Dip the baby roots in a root stimulating powder or solution, and plant it carefully in your growth medium. I would probably opt to leave them longer and make sure they are sturdy before transplanting. *Be careful not to touch the stems in the process.* I've made that mistake and it never ends well.

A second way involves taking cuttings or clonings, and inserting them directly into the growth medium. Basil and mint both do well with this method. General principles include using a very sharp knife and cutting at an angle. Dip the cut end in rooting powder and insert it into the growth medium. Watch for it to take off, and don't get impatient. As long as your leaves haven't wilted and died, there is yet hope.

Some plants can be propagated from their parents. Endive, for example, is easy to do. Cut off the bottom of a head of endive, and put it in water. New plants will grow from the base, and you can transplant these cuttings into your growth medium. I find this more of a conversational oddity than a viable way to grow my veggies. In my experience, the new head of Romaine is smaller and takes up all the growing space of a full-sized plant. Children enjoy watching the process, though, so if you have littles, go for it!

Another popular form, especially for new gardeners, is purchasing starter plants from a local nursery. This is the third way to acquire plants. Before you capitulate and do that, though, give yourself a chance. I like to take a wet paper towel, cast lettuce seed on it, fold it over and stick it in a cool dark place for a few days. When the little darlings germinate, I dip them in a rooting solution and put them in the growth medium.

I'm a diehard seed grower, and it's still my go-to for accumulating plants for any kind of garden. I pore over seed catalogs and order my seeds before Christmas. In January I start them in trays of soil or plug trays. I keep them in the dark until the first leaves appear, and then add grow lights. When the first true leaves appear, the third and fourth leaves on the plant, I transplant them into a place they can call home for a couple months. Pinch back growth to make a bushier plant. Run your hands over your tomato seedlings to encourage stronger stems.

I keep them watered and seldom need to add fertilizer before they are planted or sold. In aquaponic gardening, it is important to have a strong root system before moving them to a grow bed. As before, remember you have to gently wash out the dirt, and you want the roots strong enough to handle a little manipulation.

Some aquaponic growers talk about broadcasting seed directly over the growth medium, and just placing a layer of pebbles on top of the seeds. Personally, I have not done that. It sounds easy, but I'm old school and slightly suspicious.

AQUAPONICS GARDENING

Chapter Summary

Growing your plants is the second half of the aquaponic adventure. It's my favorite part.

- Decide how you want to get or grow your plants. If you are new to gardens, obtaining plants from a nursery is the fastest and easiest route to go.

- Starting your plants from seeds takes time. Don't expect immediate gratification.

In the next chapter, you will learn how to keep all of your hard work alive and growing.

AQUAPONICS GARDENING

CHAPTER FOURTEEN

MAINTENANCE AND PEST PREVENTION

First of all, realize that most of the problems found in traditional gardens will be eliminated without the soil. Why do you think farmers rotated crops for so many years? This is especially true when it comes to growing vegetables.

Cutworms and slugs are disgusting. Period. No longer will you need to sprinkle diatomaceous earth over the soil to discourage mollusks. Fungal and bacterial diseases propagating in the soil will no longer be an issue. (It's helpful to put a paper collar around lettuce seedlings to keep caterpillars at bay, but with aquaponic gardening you don't have to worry about any of that.) Hallelujah!

Now you can stop rejoicing, although you have other things to worry about. Your aquaponic garden is a balancing act. You need a balance between the number of fish you stock, the surface area of your biofilter, and the number of plants you grow. Your success will be determined by how well you regulate that balance and maintain a healthy environment.

Think of your fish on one side of a playground teeter totter. Your plants are on the other. The beam between the two is your biofilter with its bacteria turning ammonia into nitrates. Too little surface area means not enough bacteria, which means not enough fertilizer to grow the plants, leading to ammonia toxicity, killing the fish. On the other hand, if you stock too many fish or feed them too much, your waste may not be handled by the biofilter in place and that can also cause ammonia toxicity. Too many plants and not enough fish means your fish may be fine, but your plants will not flourish. It's a living ecosystem and you're in charge.

Before you freak out, remember: you have measuring devices to keep things under control. You just have to know what your readings mean and how to use them to adjust your system.

Let's talk about three measurements:

- Nitrogen balance: Increased levels of ammonia or nitrite suggest you have a problem with your biofilter. You need increased surface area for culturing bacteria. If your nitrate level is low, you either have too many plants or not enough fish.

- Food balance: The food ratio for leafy vegetables is 40-50 $g/m^2/day$. Fruiting vegetables, like tomatoes require 50-80 g/m²/day.

- Health assessments: Each day as you feed your fish and monitor your system, look for the tell tale signs of disease. Dead fish or plants are symptoms of a system out of whack.

One of the issues you need to safeguard against is mold. Let's talk about what mold is and is not. The white calcification you sometimes see on your growth bed is not mold. Green strands are **algae**, not mold. Look up methods to prevent algae formation in the glossary, because this could be a killer for your system as well, though it won't kill your plants or spread the same way as mold.

Mold is an opportunistic pathogen grown from spores. One type is a powdery mildew that will appear on your leaves as white spots. A more serious problem is white mold, which looks fuzzy and can grow to alarming proportions if left unchecked. At first detection, it may look like a harmless speck of white fluff, but it can turn into cankers and destroy the roots of your plant.

Mold develops because of contamination. A spore is introduced into your system. The warm, moist conditions prove favorable to its growth, until it overwhelms your system. Keep a well-ventilated system in place for moving air and don't let stagnant water sit in your trays.

AQUAPONICS GARDENING

Remove infected leaves immediately. You can wash them off with hydrogen peroxide to help prevent the spread. You can also introduce beneficial bacteria like Bacillus A. One way to eliminate mold is the use of a fungicide. The Serenade garden mold control spray is a broad-spectrum fungicide.

Mold isn't the only thing that will kill your plants, however. There are also a host of pests that may attack your plants. You have an advantage if you grow your plants indoors, but insects always seem to find a way to your garden. Your first defense is a healthy plant. An unstressed plant has high levels of phosphorus in its cells, and that repels some insects. But realize ahead of time that you are putting together an artificial system, and it is vulnerable to damage from insects.

One healthy way to rid your garden of unwanted insects is to capture them using a pheromone trap. They are specific to the insect, so one kind of trap will not fix all kinds of problems. Think of it as a glue trap collecting unwanted guests, only this trap actually attracts them. Be careful in its use. You will need to keep them away from children and pets, and you will need to wash your hands after using them. If the trap is made for outdoor use, don't try to use it indoors. Read all of the product labels before trying to use one.

Another way is to manually remove offending pests. The cabbage white fly lives on the back of leaves.

Picking them off will help reduce populations, because they produce 10 to 12 generations a year. You can feed them to your fish, who love a good, high-protein morsel. You can also drop them into a jar of soapy water and flush them away. The key is removing them immediately before they have a chance to reproduce. Another organic spray is BotaniGuard. For whiteflies, spray it directly on the plants or under the leaves. For aphids, spray it into the grow medium. It may take multiple applications to eliminate your pests, and you can use it weekly afterwards to prevent further problems.

Thrips are tiny insects that both suck out plant juices from the leaves, but also carry plant viruses. About as big as a sewing needle is wide, these are hard to see. This will be a bigger issue if your garden is out of doors, as the mature insect winters in plant debris and bark. It lays its eggs in early spring, and can produce up to fifteen generations per year. Thrips will look like little slivers unless you use a magnifying glass, and then be prepared for the shock of seeing a little animal with arms and pincers dining on your leaves. You'll more easily spot their damage in silvery and white speckles on plant leaves. Left untreated, you'll more likely see a virus causing some kind of wilting on your mature plants. You can shake them off, but that may not be aggressive enough if you're looking at an infestation.

If your aquaponic garden is outside, get rid of weeds and vegetation that provide a place for them to live. Introduce beneficial insects into your garden, things like pirate bugs, ladybugs or lacewing. Watch your plants and remove diseased leaves. You can use sticky traps to catch them manually. Since you can't employ an insecticide without affecting your fish, consider using a safe product like neem oil to treat them.

Neem oil is a safe and natural deterrent for thrips. It is extracted from the neem tree, grown in India, and contains natural insecticide and antifungal properties. It is often ingested for its medicinal properties, but the EPA deemed it safe for use in farming. There is no warning for residues with repeated application. It can be used on plant leaves without fear of affecting your fish.

All of this is made more difficult due to your ecosystem. You must learn to spot and eliminate pests without poisoning your water. You may also make your own organic spray, but be careful. What you use must be good for fish, as well as for plants. The most natural sprays you can make yourself. Use chile or garlic sprays for sap-sucking insects. For mold or fungus, you can spray a solution of potassium bicarbonate.

Chapter Summary

An aquaponic garden has natural enemies, and they attack at will. From one-celled spores to insects threatening plant annihilation, you must be prepared for the worst.

- Healthy plants are your biggest defense.
- Monitor for problems and be proactive in solving them.
- Be careful not to cause a problem in solving one. Utilize organic fish-friendly methods to discourage unwanted growth.

In the next chapter, you will learn how to take what you've learned and turn it into a business. You've made an investment, let's see a return on it in the form of profits.

CHAPTER FIFTEEN

COMMERCIAL APPLICATIONS OF AQUAPONIC GARDENING

As much as you love organic produce for your own table, don't overlook the possibility of turning a little money—or a lot—in selling what you grow. As a lover of farmer's markets, both as a consumer and as a vendor, there's a whole lot of fulfillment in the process of making money from what you love.

Begin by deciding what you grow best. For us, it was vegetables more than fish. Our setup was too small to efficiently run fish through on a scale large enough to make aquaculture profitable. However, the ability to grow more in a smaller space paid off big time. We focused on lettuce bowl veggies, primarily microgreens.

The next step is finding your market. We harbored fantasies of finding restaurants and grocery stores that would contract with us for regular deliveries of our produce. That did not happen. Agribusinesses already had contracts or provided for their own needs, and breaking into that market while vegetables went bad was not an option.

For us, the farmer's market was the easiest way to get our produce to market. We paid a small amount for a weekly stall, and once shoppers learned what we had, we enjoyed weekly visits from them. We loved it.

Our best crop came from leafy greens, specifically **microgreens,** used in salads. We started with mesclun, a salad in a seed packet with two or three different greens in the mix. Over time we grew comfortable ordering our own combinations of greens and were never disappointed.

You can begin to harvest the plants when they are two to three inches tall and have well defined leaves. If you pull off leaves, be sure to harvest the plant before it bolts (forming seeds), as the leaves will become bitter. Harvest early the morning of delivery to ensure freshness. For a Famer's Market, we combined plants and/or leaves into quart-sized plastic bags. They sold out quickly and generated a great return.

Keep in mind that microgreens germinate in half the time of regular lettuce, so start your lettuce plants earlier. They all germinate in soil 50-65 degrees in temperature, so be sure to match a cooler fish with this crop.

AQUAPONICS GARDENING

Arugula is very popular and it adds a certain zing to salads. We settled on a 1:5 ratio. For every five regular lettuce varieties, we grew one arugula. The average shopper tasting arugula will turn up his/her nose, but tasting it inside a salad, will love the way it sharpens the overall flavor.

One part of our mix was always endive (city cousin of escarole). It is very attractive in a salad, because of its deep green color and ruffled leaves. This lettuce has just a little bite to it and complements the arugula without being overpowered by it.

A third microgreen in the mix was garden cress. It has a mild flavor and you can grow either the broadleaf or curly variety for a lovely addition to the salad plate.

One of the mix was always a romaine lettuce. It takes twice as much time to germinate as the microgreens, and it needs to have larger leaves to harvest, so plan your calendar accordingly. We like to pull off individual leaves rather than trying to harvest entire heads.

Our last in the mix is a ruby lettuce, for color and texture. You'll find a lot of varieties, and we love them all. In every garden salad we sold, it was the ruby lettuce that turned heads and opened the purses.

A smaller setup can also accommodate kale. Don't leave it out of your plans. Health enthusiasts clamor for it and even die hard skeptics will try it if you include a recipe, and be happy to come back for more.

Learn how to stagger your crops. Most of your greens can be planted every three weeks to ensure an ongoing harvest. How does this translate into profit? You can expect anywhere from $15 to $20 US dollars per square foot of aquaponic gardening. Remember that you can grow plants densely per square foot, since the roots don't spread through the soil and need all that space to absorb nutrients.

We didn't sell many harvested herbs, and for good reason. For one thing, once harvested, their shelf life is very limited. Second, not many people are accustomed to cooking with fresh herbs. For the sake of convenience and economy, most buy dried herbs at their local supermarkets and are content with that.

Aquaponic gardening is by far the most productive way to earn some cash from your garden. Enjoy it as a hobbyist and let it grow naturally into a commercial enterprise. As you are ready to transition, you'll need to draw up a business plan with a financial statement that includes your cash flow, the cost of broadening your enterprise and how you plan on marketing your produce. Many limit their enterprises to one or two crops and market those as specialty items. It eliminates the need for meeting so many different requirements of large and small vegetables, and some items offer higher returns than others. Do your research and decide exactly what you want to sell and how to sell it.

Be sure to apply for and obtain your certification for organically grown produce. This means organic seeds, and no pesticides, chemicals, or artificial fertilizers. This is easy when your garden is aquaponic.

Look into obtaining a business license and make sure you have a bank account for dedicated funds. Registering your business legally makes it easier to conduct it without problems later. No matter where you live, there will be statutes regulating the growing or selling of your produce. Knowing those laws and being in compliance saves hefty fees and heartache later on.

To make this a profitable venture, you need to keep track of your costs:

Output	Cost
Plants	
Plants	
Plants	
Plants	
Plants	
Vendor Fees	
Utility/Maintenance Costs	
Total Costs	
Sales	
Bottom Line (subtract sales from costs)	

Keep a record of your building costs, and extrapolate them over a two or three season period to determine ultimate profitability. You need to recoup your costs, but it doesn't have to be in one year. Your system will last a long time, and you'll be depreciating it in your taxes over ten years, so prorate your initial investment over that same period of time.

As with any business, network with your community. Join a local Chamber of Commerce. Talk to other gardeners. You never know where your next great lead will come from, so don't limit yourself. You can learn as much from your potential buyers as from other growers. Get to know your customers.

Don't forget that the scarcity of great greens in the winter months is like money in the bank for you. Having your system productive just as local farmers get blown away by frigid temperatures or snowstorms is a plus for you.

Last but not least, consider adopting a model like the Community Supported Agriculture (CSA) type of initiative. Local customers buy shares of your produce in the planting stage. In return, they get to take part in making decisions on what to grow and also earn a percentage of the harvest. You enjoy the profit of invested money and lower the risk of loss. They enjoy the fresh produce without doing any of the work in growing it. This is a win/win situation.

Be ready to explain the benefits of your business plan:

- Locally grown and sold produce reduces food miles. This is a term describing the distance food has traveled from harvest to market shelf. Locally grown produce uses less gasoline, reducing reliance on outside markets and on fossil fuels.

- It encourages local enterprise. Utilizing sustainable practices and obtaining organic certification, you demonstrate a model others can emulate.

- It promotes genetic integrity. Growing organic seeds, especially heirloom seeds, preserves the diversity of our produce.

- It keeps local money within the community.

- It lowers food costs for the community. Locally grown food incurs less overhead and can be marketed at a savings for local families.

- It forms alliances with other small businesses, particularly restaurants. In the process, all benefit from the increased connectivity.

- It brings families and communities together. Food is a great climate for conversation and for friendship.

Be realistic and know what the critics will say before you float your idea and look for financial backing. Depending on your resourcefulness and ingenuity, it can be costly to set up a system large enough to earn an adequate salary. Some large scale commercial enterprises range from $2000 to $10,000 for their startup investment. Someone somewhere will suggest this, and you need a solid explanation for why your system won't be nearly that expensive.

Aquaponics uses up a lot of power, so factor that cost into your business plan. Do you have any energy alternatives you can utilize? What will you do when the power goes out?

An aquaponic garden is not portable. What will you do if you need to move it at some point in time? That, and aquaponic gardening needs some daily maintenance. Are you a person who follows through on your commitments? An aquaponic garden requires you know your fish and your food intimately—do you? I'm not trying to be hard-nosed here, just realistic. Any banker who is being asked to front you $5,000 to start your business is going to ask these same questions.

When you have your business outline and you can answer any curve ball with an intelligent response, you're ready to expand your hobby to the big leagues.

AQUAPONICS GARDENING

Chapter Summary

An aquaponic garden is ideal for a commercial enterprise. You are able to grow a denser crop and harvest organic produce easily.

- The easiest crop for a hobby gardener is a lettuce bowl medley.
- Keep track of costs to see if this is a profitable venture for you.
- Develop a business plan if you want to expand this into a full time business.

In the next chapter, you will learn how to prepare some of the foods you may not be accustomed to right now. It's always good to salivate (oops, I meant dream) over the good food coming your way.

AQUAPONICS GARDENING

CHAPTER SIXTEEN

MAKE GREAT FOOD

No book on aquaponic gardening would be complete without enticing you with the promise of wonderful food and tempting recipes. Assuming you aren't growing orchids and roses, you may be interested in the practical aspect of feeding you and your family. There is something innately wholesome about freshly grown food, and my hope is to inspire you to try your hand.

Fresh food offers several benefits.

- First and foremost, fresh vegetables contain all of the vitamins and minerals they are meant to have as nature's food boosters. Vegetables retrieved from cans lose so much of their innate vitality in the preservation process and in the cooking process. Even eating healthy vegetables purchased from a local market results in declining nutritional values with each hour it sits in transit and at the market. For this reason, it's healthier to grow and pick your own as you prepare dinner.

- Foods picked ahead of their normal harvest dates to be delivered to local markets lose much of their flavor in preservation or in early harvest. In short, freshly grown food is simply delicious.
- Your produce will be preservative and pesticide free.
- Your food will build bridges and memories within the family and community. People remember sitting around a table, visiting and sharing recipes. Build the life you want to live.

Much of your garden produce can be saved for winter consumption. Root vegetables can be stored in a cool, dry place and complemented with fresh herbs. This lowers your grocery bills and provides a nice variety to the fresh vegetables you're growing in your aquaponic garden.

You can extend your meals with bits and pieces of what you grow. Add extra vegetables to bulk your menu, while boosting its nutritional value. Leftover scraps of tomatoes and peppers are great in omelettes. Bits of veggies taste great in soups or stews. I cook extra tomatoes down into sauce and freeze it if I'm not making spaghetti or some other Italian dish right away.

A tremendous savings takes place when you grow and use your own produce. Here are some recipes I'd love to share with you. They represent many a meal around our table, and hope you enjoy them as well.

Simple Salad with Vinaigrette

Lettuce greens
2 slices bacon, cut into small pieces

Vinaigrette

1 Tbsp Dijon Mustard
Splash of dry white wine
¼ cup of vinegar (balsamic, walnut, etc.)
¼ cup vegetable oil
½ cup extra virgin olive oil
1 Tbsp cream

1. Prepare your salad bowl of mixed greens, tearing large pieces into bite-sized morsels.
2. Sautee bacon in a hot pan with a splash of olive oil.
3. Liquefy your mustard with a splash of dry white wine in a small mixing bowl.
4. Whisk the vegetable oil into your mustard.
5. Whisk in the olive oil when the mustard has been emulsified. (Olive oil gets bitter when whipped.)
6. Add cream at the end.

Combine your greens with the bacon pieces, pour vinaigrette on top, and toss.

Herbed Vinegars

- Use any flavor of vinegar you prefer. A nice apple cider, red wine, or balsamic vinegar are my favorites. Apple cider vinegars marry themselves well with fruit infusions, while a nice balsamic or red wine vinegar complements stronger flavors.

- Use two to three sprigs of fresh herbs
1. Place two cups of vinegar into a sterile quart canning jar.
2. Add 2-3 sprigs of fresh herbs. I love a combination of basil, rosemary and thyme.
3. Place a square of waxed paper over the top and seal with a ring.
4. Shake and let it develop rich flavor for a month. Shake every now and then. The vinegar will corrode a jar seal, so be sure to keep your waxed paper in place.

Pesto

2 cups basil
2 cloves garlic
¼ cup pine nuts
⅔ cups extra virgin olive oil
salt and pepper

Place all ingredients into a blender and run until smooth.

Use the pesto to garnish cooked pasta or fish.

Salsa

Chopped tomatoes
1 peeled and chopped mango
1 peeled and cubed avocado
½ cup minced fresh cilantro
½ cup rinsed black beans
½ cup chopped red onion

3 or 4 peeled and chopped jalapeno peppers (wear gloves)
3 Tbsp freshly squeezed lime juice
1 Tbsp extra virgin olive oil
2 cloves minced garlic
½ tsp salt.

Mix all ingredients in a bowl. I eyeball the tomatoes and taste it until I have the right ratio. Let it chill before using it as a garnish or serving with chips.

Sauteed Vegetable Plate

Equal portions sliced carrots, whole green beans, colorful peppers, onion
Splash extra virgin olive oil
Splash dry white wine
Splash balsamic vinegar
Handful dried cranberries
Handful sliced almonds
1 Tbsp butter

1. Heat a large skillet and then melt the butter. Add the almonds and lightly toast them. Remove the walnuts and return the skillet to the stove.
2. Heat your skillet once again and add your olive oil.
3. When the oil starts to flow like water, add your sliced vegetables.
4. Sear your vegetables, then toss and let them get crispy around the edges.
5. Add the white wine; scrape up the pan's little pieces.
6. Add the craisins, and let warm until they are soft.

7. Add the almonds. Stir slightly, and pour the mixture into a serving bowl.

Flamed-Kissed Grilled Veggies

Our family loves an outdoor gathering in the spring, summer, and fall. We often throw a bowl of tossed veggies on the side of the grill, and if we want to be formal, thread them onto skewers. Remember that wooden skewers need to be soaked in water to prevent them from catching on fire. I've made that mistake once before! Most usually I toss them into a grill basket and set them directly on the grill.

Here's my bouquet of grilled produce.

Garlic: 30 minutes for a whole head. Set the garlic bulb on foil and drizzle with extra virgin olive oil and a sprinkle of salt.. Wrap it in foil and pinch the top closed.

Onions: 25 minutes. Peel and cut into quarters.

Peppers: 20 minutes. Cut into halves or quarters and remove the seeds.

Potatoes: 15 minutes. Slice into ¼ inch pieces. Parboil for a couple minutes. Drain and coat them with extra virgin olive oil, sprinkle salt and pepper.

Green beans: 10 minutes. Snap off the ends.

Squash: 10 minutes. Cut into large chunks.

Lettuce: 5 to 10 minutes. A head of Romaine works well. Char it lightly, but don't cook it all the way through.

Tomatoes: 5 minutes. Cut into chunks or quarters.

Your veggies will be fork tender when they are done.

Garden Fresh Minestrone Soup

Parboil a dried bean bouquet. I like a combination of navy beans and pinto beans. Simmer them in four quarts of vegetable or chicken stock for an hour or two. Drain your beans in a colander and rinse them. (I know you'll lose your B vitamins by rinsing them, but you'll also lose the gas, and your family will thank you.) Add your freshly shelled beans and cook for another hour or so, until all of the beans are tender. I usually figure about four to five cups of cooked beans are a good base. Set them aside in a bowl.

Soup ingredients:

3 Tbsp butter
4 large, chopped onions
10 garlic cloves, finely minced
1 mildly hot or flavorful pepper, finely diced
2 chopped sweet peppers
6 to 8 large tomatoes, chopped, with juices

AQUAPONICS GARDENING

½ cup dry white wine
1 cup diced carrots
2 cups corn kernels
3 cups cooked pasta of choice
3 cups kale

Seasoning bouquet:

2 tsp savory
1 tsp oregano
½ tsp rosemary
½ tsp thyme
salt and pepper to taste

1. Melt the butter in a large skillet and saute the onion and garlic. Add peppers and cook until all veggies are soft.
2. Add the white wine, stirring up all the crispy little pieces of veggies.
3. Add tomatoes and increase the heat, stirring, reducing the mixture for about five minutes.
4. Move your sauteed mix into the bean pot. Add all your seasonings.
5. Add the rest of your veggies, and cooked pasta. Let them simmer for about 20 minutes, mixing all those luscious flavors.
6. Chop your kale and add in the last five minutes before serving.
7. Garnish with minced flat leaf parsley and basil.

Fish Under Cover

Fish
3 lb fish fillets
2 Tbsp butter
1 onion, peeled and chopped
1 clove minced garlic
1 Tbsp chicken bouillon or fish paste
1 tsp black pepper
¼ cup dry white wine

Filling
2 sticks butter
1 ¼ cup flour
3 cups hot chicken broth
1 cup warmed cream
small handful crushed thyme leaves
2 large carrots cut into coins and cooked until tender
1 cup peas

Crust
2 cups sifted flour
1 tsp salt
⅔ cup cold butter
4-5 Tbsp cold water

For the fish: Melt your butter in a skillet until it bubbles. Add the onion and garlic, cook until transparent. Add the crushed bouillon or fish paste, stirring. Lay the cod on your bed of vegetables and add the white wine. Let simmer on low as the fish cooks.

AQUAPONICS GARDENING

For the filling: In a medium saucepan, melt the butter over medium heat until it is foamy. Add the flour a bit at a time, creating a roux. Let it brown slightly. Stir in chicken broth a little at a time, constantly whisking. Add the thyme leaves as it bubbles and thickens. Add the cooked carrots and peas.

For the crust: Put the flour and salt into a mixing bowl, and stir to mix. Cut in the cold butter. Add the water, stir, then turn out on pastry sheet. Roll out the bottom crust and lay it in a pie plate. Add the fish and then pour the creamy filling. Roll out and lay the second crust on top of the pie. Create vent holes for steam and crimp edges.

Bake the fish pie at 425 degrees for 35-40 minutes.

Rib-Sticking Pasta Salad

Salad Bed
2 medium zucchini, sliced
2 cups peas
1 head broccoli, cut into florets
¼ cut green onions, sliced
2 cloves minced garlic
1 lb cooked bowtie pasta

Dressing
¼ herbed vinegar

¼ cup honey
¼ cup freshly squeezed lemon juice
2 Tbsp chopped chives
2 Tbsp minced flat leaf Italian parsley
3 Tbsp dijon mustard
Splash dry white wine
salt and pepper to taste

Topper:

2 cups cooked fish, poached in white wine and seasoned with a handful of thyme.

Prepare the **Dressing**
1. Liquefy your mustard with a splash of dry white wine in a small mixing bowl.
2. Whisk the vinegar and honey into the mustard mixture.
3. Add the herbs and spices.

Toss the vegetables with the cooked, cooled pasta.
Add the dressing and toss to coat well.
Lay the fish on top of the bed of pasta.

Fish Cakes

6 Tbsp butter, divided
1 small onion, minced
2 cloves minced garlic
1 pound fresh fish, chopped
¼ cup mayonnaise
1 large egg, slightly beaten
1 Tbsp Dijon mustard
1 Tbsp soy sauce

1 Tbsp lemon juice
¼ tsp hot sauce
Salt and pepper
3 cups breadcrumbs, divided into one cup and two cups

1. Melt 2 Tbsp butter in a large skillet.
2. Add the onion and garlic, cook until tender, remove from heat.
3. Place the sauteed vegetables in a bowl with the fish pieces.
4. Add the whisked egg and mayonnaise, stirring.
5. Add all the seasonings, stirring.
6. Add 2 cups of bread crumbs, stirring.
7. Fashion the mixture into eight fish cakes.
8. Coat each cake with the last of the bread crumbs.
9. Melt the remaining butter in the skillet. Let it sizzle and get foamy.
10. Lay the cakes into the butter and cook over medium-high heat 4 to 5 minutes on each side, until golden and fish is cooked.
11. Remove from skillet and pat with paper towels.

Sweet Corn Relish:

4 cups corn
2 large chopped tomatoes
3 green onions, sliced
¼ tsp herbed vinegar

Toss the vegetables together with the vinegar and garnish the fish cakes.

Chilli Rellenos with White Fish

1 lb cooked fish pieces
2 Tbsp butter
½ cup chopped onion
1-2 cups chopped green chilis
2 tsp marjoram
1 tsp cumin
1 ½ cup cream
¼ cup flour
4 beaten eggs
2 cups shredded cheese.

1. Melt the butter, adding the onion and chilies. Cook until tender.
2. Coat a baking dish with butter.
3. Mix the flour and cream until smooth. Add the eggs and beat well. Stir in spices.
4. Fold the cooked fish into the creamy mixture.
5. Pour the creamy mixture into prepared baking dish.
6. Top with cheese.
7. Bake at 350 degrees for 45-50 minutes, until a knife comes out clean.
8. Let it stand five minutes before serving.

Seafood Crepes

Filling:
2 Tbsp butter
2 Tbsp flour
¼ to ½ cup dry white wine
Chopped sage or basil or marjoram
Chunks of white fish.

1. Melt the butter and stir in the flour.
2. Let the roux brown before adding wine. Whisk.

3. Add the spices and the fish, and cover with a tight fitting lid. Let the seafood cook. When it is cooked through, remove it from the heat.

Crepe:

1 cup flour
1 ⅓ cup liquid, comprised of milk and water
¼ tsp salt
3 Tbsp butter

1. Mix the flour, liquid and seasoning in a blender and refrigerate.
2. Melt the butter in the skillet until it dances.
3. Pour ½ cup of mixture into the pan and tip the pan so it fills the bottom.
4. Let it brown, flip it, and when the second side is brown, lift it out.
5. Lay it on a plate with a layer of waxed paper between each crepe.

When the crepes are cooked, lay one on each plate. Add filling and roll it. Garnish with a sprig of rosemary.

AQUAPONICS GARDENING

PART IV

THE SCIENCE BEHIND AQUAPONIC GARDENING

CHAPTER SEVENTEEN

GLOSSARY OF TERMS

aerating pump — All of God's creatures need oxygen, and fish are no exception. A little explanation of how your fish will use it illustrates the importance of supplying this basic life sustaining element. Fish may not have lungs, but they still need air to breathe, filtering dissolved oxygen from the water through their gills.

The gills (usually four on each side) are situated just behind the head, and are a series of bony flaps with filaments. Just as the human bronchus divides again and again to form a pulmonary tree for oxygen intake and exchange, the gill filaments support a network of lamellae. Water runs through the gills and those busy little filaments employ osmotic action to extract oxygen from the water with carbon dioxide being released in the exchange. That precious life sustaining oxygen is directly absorbed into the fish's bloodstream.

Atmospheric oxygen comprises about 20% of the air we breathe, but that number is significantly reduced when we talk about dissolved oxygen in a fish tank. The amount of dissolved oxygen in the water decreases as the water temperature rises. Take a look at Chapter Ten, in which the water temperatures for various fishes are listed. At 59 degrees Fahrenheit the water will absorb less than 5% of the oxygen available from the air, 4.35% to be exact. That figure decreases for every degree of temperature as the water warms. Hence the need for an aeration pump.

How do you choose one? I'm glad you asked. Here are some of my top picks:

The Tetra Easy Whisper Air Pump is an excellent choice. Its manufacturer claims its quiet sound is a result of its domed surface reducing the noise of the engine. If your tank is clear and you want to enjoy your fish as they swim around, this one will provide bubbles to increase your viewing pleasure. It comes with a lifetime guarantee, which is a plus if you're not wanting to fix a breakdown yourself.

It comes in five graduated sizes for whatever scale you have designed for your fish tank. The company reviews are not the best, but check out the website for yourself.

The Hygger 16mm air pump is another great option. It is quiet, and appropriate for a tank up to six feet deep, pumping 16 L/min of air. It comes with just a one year warranty, is not recommended for use out of doors, and should not get wet.

The Active Aqua air pump is seven inches in diameter and not submersible. It offers a lot of aeration and is fairly quiet, and comes with a detailed set of instructions for installation. The system is energy efficient, but don't use it if your aquaponic garden is out of doors.

For a smaller tank (50-160 gallons), the Fluval q2 pump is a good alternative. It is low maintenance and inexpensive to set up, although you will need an aerator for the tank. It is designed with a dual wall chamber to muffle noise, has replaceable diaphragms, and circulates 25 L/min in air flow.

A fifth great option is the Mylivell pump. It is not waterproof and attaches via a suction cup to the outside of your tank. It is low voltage and runs with no motor, making it one of the quietest options available. This is suitable for a smaller set up.

Be aware that many of these don't come with tubing, so read the fine print to be sure you have everything you need when it's time to install it.

algae — Those nasty green strands in your tank are quite a nuisance, but worse, they can destroy your aquaponic garden. Algae are organisms growing in your water. Some are just single-celled organisms, and others grow in colonies creating chloroplasts as they grow. Left unchecked, they can cloud your water and make it feel foul. Worse, algae affects your pH level and uses precious oxygen in their growth.

Let's look at the oxygen issues first. Your fish need oxygen, and the last thing you want is to find them asphyxiated one morning due to oxygen depletion through the night. How does that happen, and what does algae have to do with it? Like all plants, algae will produce oxygen during daily photosynthesis. At night, when there is no light for photosynthesis, these strands will start to use your tank's reservoir of dissolved oxygen for their own growth, resulting in lower levels for your fish. If your fish appear to be suffering despite high oxygen levels, check your readings during the middle of the night. You may find them extremely low. Worse yet, when algae begins to die, the cells consume oxygen to decompose and further deplete your oxygen reservoir.

Algae also affects your delicate pH balance. These, as in photosynthesis, relate to the rising and the setting of the sun, and are called diurnal swings. As algae consume CO_2 during the day, they raise the water pH, making it more basic. The readings fluctuate based on when photosynthesis ends, and your water pH will lower, becoming more acidic. Keeping your system in balance becomes tricky and time-consuming.

AQUAPONICS GARDENING

The best solution lies in preventing it. Make sure you maintain proper pH and oxygen levels in your water and make sure your pump keeps water moving without stagnation. Look at your water's phosphorus level. If you see it begin, try to control the amount of growth. Shading your water will decrease its formation, since algae needs sunlight to grow.

Filtration also helps. If you have the ingenuity and time to put together the filters, screens, and devices to remove uneaten food, waste and decaying plants, you can prevent the buildup of algae. Depending on what kind of filter you use, you'll cycle your water through pads, sponges, or wool to snag the waste before it is returned to the tank. You'll need to periodically clean your filter. Take it from the tank, clean it in clear water, and quickly return it, turning everything on again. One caveat: Use something other than tap water so you don't kill your cultured bacteria.

In addition to mechanical filtration, systems employing chemicals are also available. Buying a system can be expensive, but you have to counter that against the cost of losing your crop or seeing your fish die. Which scenario do you want to manage? I have found the purchase of a filtration system more valuable than trial and error, and favor mechanical systems over biological or chemical strategies.

An aquarium filter pad in one easy option. It is adaptable to any size or shape required, and inexpensive. You'll need to replace it every three to four weeks, so establish a regimen and way to keep track of time.

Another method utilizes activated charcoal, which comes in pellets. You can grind it to the size of product you want, using either the pellets or reducing it to a fine powder. It works quickly and efficiently, and is less unsightly.

A third option is a reusable medium that functions in a different way. These are shaped like tiny little hexagrams to increase the surface area of water to filtration media, and function very efficiently.

Look at all of the products available and read reviews to select the one you wish to use. The point is to be proactive and reduce algae immediately. Cleaning your tank keeps your fish healthy and your water levels within normal limits.

biofilter — You'll hear this term a lot in aquaponic gardening, but it isn't complicated. A biofilter serves to extend your bed of microbes, converting fish waste to plant food. Yes, it's really that simple. It becomes an important consideration when you are submerging your plants into the water rather than cultivating them in a growth medium like hydroton pellets.

AQUAPONICS GARDENING

If you have a large operation with a raft of bedding plants and surface water to spare, you can utilize a floating medium like K1 media to increase the surface area of microbes and provide adequate fertilization. You can also install static trays or drip filters and cycle your water through them between the solid waste filter and the submerged plants.

Your need for a biofilter is determined by the density of your fish population relative to the volume of water, as well as how many plants you want to grow. If you maintain a small number of fish and don't overfeed them, you are going to be producing less solid waste and may be able to get by without a biofilter.

deep water culture — This growing technique involves a deeper water supply with floating plants that rest on the surface, their roots submerged in the water. It alleviates the need for canals or tubes, pumping the water through a series of tanks, and is scalable from the tiniest of ambitions to large rafts of plants grown for commercial purposes.

ebb and flow — This system of watering and feeding your plants is centuries old, and remains one of the simplest forms of aquaponic today. It is also known as a flood and drainage system. You will create your "flood table" by growing produce in a plastic tray with your growth medium positioned above the tank reservoir. Several times each day your sump pump is turned on to pump your watery stew up a pipe, emptying into your grow tray. Let it sit there and drain slowly until the next scheduled flooding/feeding for your plants. You can install a timer to handle the process automatically.

fish food — What food and how much of it are you going to be getting? Nelson Pade offers a great organic, non-GMO food for fish, available in small or large bags online. You can also buy fish food from local pet stores or a nearby WalMart. What you feed fish is determined by the type of fish you're growing, but realize a few basic things. First, when you buy any kind of fish food, it will be loaded with a good mix of nutrients, a balance of protein, carbs, fats, and minerals. That's why it's so expensive.

Others opt for making their own. If you're wanting to reduce costs, try duckweed, digging worms from the backyard, or slipping some larvae into your tank. If your fish are picky and won't eat these delicacies, you'll have to gather the remains to avoid excess strain on your filters.

genetically modified organisms — Agribusinesses began experimenting with ways to improve on Mother Nature and devised ways of modifying the genetic structure of the food we eat. Their good intentions of reducing food shortages unleashed a storm of controversy over the benefits versus the harms of ingesting GMOs.

AQUAPONICS GARDENING

The rise in food-based allergies has risen from 3.4% in the late nineties to more than 5% in 2011. There is no evidence that genetically modified foods are responsible, but there is no evidence that it's not, either. The rising incidence of cancer worldwide, along with the increased development of superbugs, all provide fodder for the arguments against genetically modified foods. Again, there is no proof either way, but might I just suggest that it's not natural?

grow lights — Who has enough sunlight for an indoor aquaponic garden? Not many of us. Luckily, you have choices, and you have three main considerations. First, look at its size to be sure it will meet your garden's needs. Second, look at how it attaches. Some screw into existing light sockets and others are mounted to the ceiling. Third, look at the light's features. What color light does it put out? Does it require regulating? Is it noisy? Most importantly, what kind of heat does it put out? I know. It sounds like way too much complication for something as simple as light, but nothing is simple when it comes to aquaponic gardening. This is science, people

The Feit hanging light is adaptable to either a flush or suspended attachment, and you can get various sizes ranging from 5 inches to 2 feet in diameter. It runs on 120 V electrical power and comes with a 2-year warranty. Be aware that it has a 5 foot cord, so take that into consideration.

This bamboo suspended light is affordable and offers the convenience of being scalable. You can stack them for expanding applications. The LED lights are economical and do not require adjustment as your plants grow. They are great for a small setup.

If you need a larger system, look at the Philizon system of lighting, made in China. These range from a smaller version available on Amazon as a 600 LCD variety, up to multiple bars for extensive growing.

herbs — These are great for aquaponic gardens, because unlike vegetables, you are growing small amounts to flavor dishes rather than whole meals.

Culinary herbs grow in a lot of different ways. Some are perennials, some look like small shrubs, and others like small trees. Thyme, sage, lavender, parsley, basil, rosemary, and bay are the most commonly grown herbs. There are over four hundred medicinal herbs you can grow, but it requires knowing how to use the herb. Some are steeped into teas. Some can be applied topically. Others may be ingested, but it isn't an exact science.

I'm a lover of the idea of homeopathic healing, but never courageous enough to grow my own and self-medicate. My recommendation: grow what you'll use to season your food.

AQUAPONICS GARDENING

high tunnel — This is a structure built and covered with plastic. It serves as a mini greenhouse and can be either a simple protective covering or a fancy one with installed watering systems, fans, and a heat source. Homesteaders have been jumping on the high tunnel bandwagon, and with good reason. Also known as hoophouses, these unheated structures extend the growing season. Both hobby gardeners and commercial growers have embraced them, especially since the USDA started their high tunnel initiative. They come in many different sizes and configurations, ranging from 1000 square feet to hooking several together, spanning multiple acres.

homeostasis — Simply defined, it is the process of supporting life by maintaining a balance of neutrality within the body or organism. If you can understand the process in your own body, you have a frame of reference for understanding what is happening in your aquaponic garden. Your body employs many compensatory mechanisms for maintaining the ideal blood sugar, blood pressure, body temperature, cellular water level, and pH, to name a few.

Your ideal body pH is 7.35 to 7.45. Within this narrow range, you are running your engines on all four cylinders. Suppose you start to hyperventilate. Your body will blow off carbon dioxide (CO_2), which is an acid, in each breath. That loss of CO_2 will make your blood more alkaline, lowering your blood pH. To compensate, your kidneys will kick in, excreting bicarb

(HCO_3), which is alkaline, and voila, your blood pH returns to a level within its normal range.

hydroponics — Literally, this means growing plants in water. Because many of the same principles are employed in an aquaponic garden, remember, one part of the word is derived from *hydroponic*, let's look at your options. Get a firm understanding of these principles before designing your system.

Six types of hydroponic gardens may be constructed, and the first three require more ingenuity, or trial and error, than the latter three.

- The wick system is used by inserting a wick (think of a candle wick) into the plant container, which draws the water up to feed and water the roots.
- A water culture system employs lightweight containers holding plants that float in the water, directly absorbing the chemically laden water.
- An ebb and flow system requires immersing one plant in water and then draining it into from one to the other, and so on. It requires a pumping mechanism to regulate the flow of water.
- A drip system requires a pump with a timer, which as you would guess, drips water onto the plants at appropriate intervals.

AQUAPONICS GARDENING

- A nutrient film is used in both hydroponic and aquaponic gardening, pumping the chemically fertilized water constantly through the roots.

hydroton — These little gems are a form of dried clay broken up and baked into small pellets. If you've ever rooted plants in a glass of water, you know that the plant languishes against the side of the glass because its stem has no support of its own. Your plants need some sort of structure for growing straight and tall. The most often source in aquaponic gardening is hydroton pellets.

Most gardening centers offer bags of vermiculite and other soil-based media in large displays. Before entering the world of aquaponic gardening, I wasn't familiar with it either, but I soon learned it offered five benefits:

1. The little pellets are filled with tiny pores, and they are like sponges growing on the ocean floor. They absorb water, but drain out excess if you use them in a soil-based application. For our purposes, they hold water and provide surface area for necessary bacterial growth.
2. These clay baked pellets hold their shape over time, not needing to be replaced as often, and allowing your plant roots to continuously exchange nitrogen to oxygen.
3. The pellets maintain the proper acid/base balance in your garden.

4. The pellets are produced in gigantic kilns and the high temperature results in a sterile product. You want to grow your own bacteria, not introduce microbes toxic for either plants or fish into the mix.
5. Hydroton pellets are reusable. You can rinse them out and use them over and over again. What a bargain!

LECA aggregates — There are a number of grow media out there. All of the pebbles in this category will work for you. You'll need small net pots 1.5 to 2.5 inches in diameter. Soak your pebbles and place seeds on top, covering them with one or two water-soaked pebbles, depending on recommended planting depth. Hydroton is a brand of pellets, usually manufactured by heating clay in a rotating kiln. As it heats, the clay expands and forms pellets with incredibly increased surface areas for cultivating the bacteria you need as a growth medium.

When you open the package, soak them for 4 to 6 hours to remove dust, as well as to be sure they won't float in your system. Some forms will not be good for the pH of your water. How do you tell? Do a vinegar test. Put a small handful of pellets in a glass of vinegar. If bubbles rise to the surface, it has too much limestone in its composition and won't work for your system. Always look for smaller pellets, because the larger ones have more air space. You're wanting the highest porous surface area possible.

AQUAPONICS GARDENING

media bed — This system will look more like traditional gardening, since larger pots or trays hold the LECA (Lightweight Expanded Clay Aggregate) pellets, and the plant grows looking like its traditional counterpart. The bed needs to be about 12 inches deep, and it increases the cost substantially.

The container you choose may be the most important decision you'll make. It will take up the largest amount of space, and it will need a depth best suited for the plants you want to grow. Fill it with pebbles, usually Hydroton, to within two inches of the top. Remember that 12 inches is recommended. This grow bed acts as the biofilter.

If you are building a tower system with PVC pipes as your gardening bed, you're going to be investing in a lot more pellets. Don't skimp here. Less is not more, more is more.

nitrogen cycle — This is the process sustaining life on planet earth. While nitrogen in its gaseous state comprises about 87% of our atmosphere, its life-sustaining qualities are not accessible by our bodies in its gaseous state.

1. Scientists call the first step in the cycle nitrogen fixation. Bacteria convert fish waste into ammonia. Ammonia (if you remember back to chemistry class) is chemically known NH_3, and the process of nitrification begins.

2. In nitrification, bacteria transform NH_3 to NO_3, which plants utilize as a nitrate fertilizer.

In aquaponic gardening, the most important part of this cycle of life isn't either the fish or the plants. It's the growth medium. The Nitrogen Cycle takes place on the growth medium, most often hydroton pellets, where the nitrifying bacteria find a home and carry out this important part of the process.

nutrient film — A nutrient film is a thin layer of nutrient-rich water that flows through plant roots for absorption. In hydroponic watering systems (which aquaponics is, merely replacing fish with chemicals), the water is distributed in channels, often without the aid of pumps. The slope of the channel, the rate at which the water flows, and the right size of the channelling system, work together to create this perfect system for healthy plant growth. You'll read about wicking and ebb and flow in hydroponic gardening, but don't get overwhelmed. We eliminate the mystique in aquaponic gardening by using a small pump, which eliminates the need for a degree in physics, resulting in water being distributed automatically.

organic gardening — Organic gardening is pure and unadulterated growth of plants without chemical fertilizers, herbicides, or pesticides. Many claim that these have been linked to breast cancer, damaged brain function, Parkinson's disease, miscarriages, birth defects, autism, prostate cancer, non-Hodgkin's lymphoma, and infertility. Please realize a link is not definitive proof of causation, but it's enough to make a thinking person go, "Hmmm." There are other benefits as well. Many believe the compounded toxicity of constantly pouring chemicals into our soil, worldwide, will be catastrophic in years to come. Aquaponics offers a 100% organic gardening experience.

pH balance — Maintaining a neutral acid/base balance in your water is a matter of regulating the chemical reactions taking place. This is achieved, in part, by the nitrogen cycle, and nitrification forms the chemical basis for sustaining the aquatic and plant life in your aquaponic garden. Here's how the cycle is played out in your little microcosm of underwater drama. Your fish eat and convert their ingested proteins into ammonia (NH_3) and ammonium (NH_4+).

The ammonia in their water is toxic for the fish, so it is imperative that the process of nitrification begins to take place immediately. The normal and beneficial bacteria in your water will colonize in the media you've installed in your tank (usually clay pebbles like hydroton). One of those beneficial bacteria is nitrosomonas, and it chemically transforms the ammonia into ammonium by combining with the oxygen you are pumping into your water through the aerator. Here's what takes place:

AQUAPONICS GARDENING

$$NH_3 + O_2 \rightarrow NO_2 + 3H^+ + 2e^-$$

This represents the first step in nitrification. The second step is the introduction of a second equally important bacteria, nitrobacter, which completes the process of turning ammonia into nitrate, i.e., plant food. Here's what takes place:

$$NO_2 + H_2O \rightarrow NO_3 + 2H^+ + 2e^-$$

Those two loose electrons are absorbed into the water, making it more acidic and thereby increasing the pH. Your test kit will measure levels of nitrate, nitrite, and ammonia within your water, so you can track the process from day to day.

photosynthesis— You heard all about this in school, but it probably went in one ear and out the other. Now, it's time to get serious and be sure you understand what's involved. You know it's a chemical process in which plants take sunlight and convert its energy into chloroplasts, keeping plants green and healthy. In this give and take reaction, water transfers electrons to carbon dioxide to produce carbohydrates. During the reaction the carbon dioxide loses electrons and the water become oxidized. The cycle is Mother Nature's way of keeping all of the plants and animals happy through mutually beneficial trades.

sump pump— Don't skimp on your pump. As you're counting the cost in building your aquaponic garden, there's always the temptation to channel your money into a fancier aquarium or into more fish. Resist that temptation. Your ecosystem will only be as good as its bones, and you need to invest in the right equipment. Here are my top five picks:

Coming in three sizes, the Fluval Hagen Sea Pumps are as good as any on the market. Its patented Smart-Pump™ technology, offered in both the SP4/SP6 models, actually monitors its efficiency and shuts off in the event of overheating. Its cool operation will not affect water temperature, a huge plus. Because it isn't metal, nothing will corrode in outdoor humidity or exposure to water in the tank. It is submersible, but can also run outside of the tank. Be aware that it's not the quietest out there, but if your system is in the basement or out of doors, that may not be a problem.

A second option to consider is the Aqueon. Noted for an adjustable flow rate, it offers you a lot more control over your new ecosystem. The manufacturers claim it is quiet, but reviewers are not 100% on this feature. It is easy to install and it is submersible, so it's suitable for an outdoor garden.

The Jebao DCP Sine Wave Submersible Pump is perfect for a larger aquaponic garden. It is submersible, powerful, and relatively quiet. It will not affect water temperature inside of your tank. It is one of five Jebao models to choose from, so do your homework and look at all of the options before making a purchase.

I am also impressed with the Eheim models. This company makes pumps for ponds as well as several options for varying sizes of aquariums. The Universal 600 comes in both a larger and more compact model. It comes with a removable prefilter and is designed for quiet efficiency. The downside? As you might expect, it's not the cheapest pump on the market. My sainted mother always said, "You only get what you pay for," and in this instance, she is right. I think it's worth the money.

My fifth fave is the Uniclife model. The DEP-400 is equipped with a memory function to store settings, handy when you want to shut it down or lower its output, making it easier to set back up again. It is manufactured with an intake screen which serves as a mini-filter to help keep out debris. The manufacturers suggest it to be run under water to keep the engine cool, but you know what that means, don't you? It will raise water temperature. On the plus side, it is energy efficient.

Do your homework. Look at the manufacturing specs, talk to people in the know. Check out pet stores, as well as professionals at Grainger. If you're building a tower of growing beds, you'll need more of a professional grade pump, so plan accordingly.

sustainability — We live in a delicate relationship with our home on Earth, and everything we do affects that relationship. When we grow and consume responsibly, nature and man live hand in hand. Our goal is to live *with* our environment. Nurture it, not plunder it. For too many years we have looked at the earth as a magical genie, stripping its natural resources with no thought of the consequences. Sustainability is a new way of looking at our earth home, and using our resources in a way that ensures future generations never get left with a bankrupt environment.

In 1969, the United States adopted The National Environmental Policy Act "to create and maintain conditions under which humans and nature can exist in productive harmony, that permit fulfilling the social, economic, and other requirements of present and future generations." To this end, the EPA established strategies that keep man and nature in balance. Two of their most ambitious and worthwhile projects have been facilitating the rising number of high tunnels and solar panels installed across the country. Rebates and information have led many a seeker to a more sustainable lifestyle. Preppers and hobbyists both benefit from their initiatives.

symbiosis — In its most basic definition, symbiosis is the process of two organisms living together. In commensalism, one organism benefits from the other (think spider webs on trees). In parasitism, one lives off

AQUAPONICS GARDENING

of the other (think tapeworms). In mutualism, both organisms benefit, as in aquaponics. Your bacteria are tiny one-celled organisms you want to nurture and give a home to, because they are exchanging the ammonia your fish excrete into valuable fertilizer for your plants. These beneficial bacteria are not causing disease or going to infect you, so no worries. This is a win/win situation for the fish and for the plants. Find symbiotic worksheets to learn more!

water testing kits — By now you realize the importance of monitoring your water. The most deluxe system will measure pH, oxygen, ammonia levels, nitrates, nitrites, general hardness and carbonate water hardness, potassium, iron, and trace elements. Let's look first at normal values.

- Your water pH needs to be between 6 and 8, with 6.5 being ideal.

- Ammonia measures read between 0.25 and 8.0 ppm of ammonia.

- A good kit will measure nitrites between 0.25 and 5.0 ppm of nitrites.

- Look for a kit that measures ranges of 5 - 160 ppm of nitrates.

- An idea kit will also measure general water hardness as well as mineral solution. The same elements that make your water hard or soft will also affect your aquarium. If you use rain water, it should not contain minerals.

- Low potassium levels in the water will affect your plants. You can doctor that with additions of potassium hydroxide, which will raise your pH without making your water hard.

- Just like you, your plants need iron to grow lush green leaves.

Bear in mind that you aren't looking for a simple jar with test strips. You're not just measuring pH like you would for a swimming pool. This is science. Be thorough. Here are some of my top picks: Nelson Padeputs out a top of the line kit. They offer detailed instructions on using the kit and have a table with normal ranges.. Did I mention it was top of the line? Watch your jaw drop when you look it up, but it is very thorough.

Another option is from the LaMott company, with more than one kit advertised. This is another high end model, but with choices to make it more affordable.

At the other end of the spectrum is the Ultimate 14 in 1 jar with test strips, available on Amazon. As you would guess, it measures fourteen different levels and requires color coded assessment. Potassium and oxygen are not in that list.

The bottom line is simple: Test your water or risk losing both your fish and your plants. You don't need the most expensive system on the planet, but investing in quality makes a difference. My sainted mother always said, "You only get what you pay for," and in the world of aquaponic garden water testing, this is certainly true.

wicking system — This is a very simple way to transport your nutrient-laden water to your plant roots. Think of the way a paper towel utilizes capillary motion to draw moisture from a kitchen countertop. If you operate a small aquaponic garden, you can implement this age old strategy.

Wicking is a passive system whereby you draw water from your tank into your growing bed. You won't need expensive pumps, and instead install wicks comprised of rope or felt which will pull water upward. Be sure to keep your water level high enough that it doesn't have to be drawn very far.

This can be adapted for a crossover system utilizing both traditional growing media and nutrient-rich aquaponic water. Prepare a bed, and install a pipe for delivering water into the base of the bed. The water travels upward to meet the plant roots without the need to water from above.

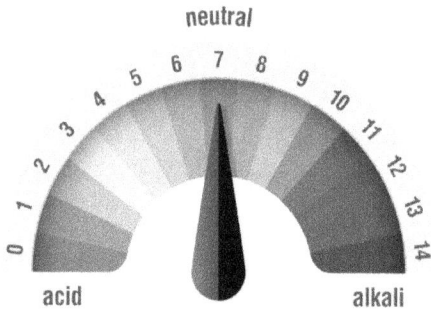

FINAL WORDS

By now you're an expert on aquaponic gardening. You've learned about what it is and isn't and you're sold on its benefits. Take a moment and list the reasons why you want to start one. See how your list compares to mine:

- Year round fresh produce
- Organic and non-GMO produce at a price I can afford
- A small side gig growing plants for others

These are all valuable reasons for diving into the world of aquaponics. If you're a prepper or survivalist, this is right up your alley. If you're a gardener, this is the best thing since sliced bread. And if you are wanting to put fresh food on the table, this book has been written for you.

We discussed in detail the concept behind aquaponic gardening. You know by now that the nitrogen cycle is your friend. Read and reread the explanations of how to grow a nutritious watery stew for plants and fish. Find a friend and explain it. If you're like me, you can read it and say, "Uh, huh. I get it." A week later it's like a vacuum in my brain sucked it all away. It's not until I read it, digest the information, and then explain it to someone else that it earns a place inside of my head. Your understanding of the concepts is the key to your success.

Be sure you understand all the readings required in using a test kit. Put together a system for tracking measurements with dates and norms in the very first column. If you have it ready, you'll use it. I know from personal experience that it's all too easy to test the water, and think. "Hmph. That's interesting. I wonder what it will be tomorrow." The next day I test the water and think, "Hmph. That's interesting." By the third day, I no longer remember the first day's readings and only a vague idea of where I've been or where I'm wanting to be. Keeping a record of your results is how you most quickly produce the optimal watery blend for your plants and it is the basis for each adjustment in the process. Don't be the haphazard you. Be the smarter you. Set up a notebook *before* you begin.

Think back over the type of aquaponic garden you're most interested in building. Do you want a simple nutrient film with either the drip or ebb and flow type of watering? Do you want a deep water culture? Is the media-based grow bed more your style? Narrowing down your system takes this from theory to practice. You are one step closer to actually following through and creating your very own aquaponic garden.

Now, take it from theory into practicality. Sketch out or refine the garden of your dreams. Are you the scrounger? The engineer? The unicorn? The beginner with a hectic lifestyle needing the convenience of a kit? There is no one way to venture through the garden gate into aquaponic gardening. No one style is superior to another. There is only you, your lifestyle, the challenges that make your heart race with pleasure. Design a garden that is you or a combo of you and your partner.

Even if the time is not now, creating a sketch is your promise to yourself, *someday. Someday I will do this.* A sketch is the basis of your shopping list. By putting it down on paper and realizing what you need to find or purchase, you have fashioned a checklist. You can watch for sales and put together a box with all your bits and pieces much more economically if you do this over time. Nothing spells defeat faster than a bottom line beyond your means. And that needn't be the case.

Decide on your fish and on your plants. This is where it all becomes a sparkle in your eye. This carries you from the fear of starting to the gigantic first step of construction. That first step is the only step that matters. I believe in the adage, *well begun is half done.* If you don't start you can't finish. It's just that simple. You have to take the first step in cutting pipes or washing gravel, some deliberate action that takes the theoretical into the physical.

Take some time creating the perfect water before you plant. You know by now that the nutrient-laden water holds the magic of growth. Don't rush through this all important step in the process. Success is what primes the system for continued growth, expanding your enterprise, dreaming of bigger and better systems. Rushing is the death knell to all of your invested time and money.

Begin experimenting with recipes. It will whet your appetite for more healthy food and encourage you to start your experiment. Collect other recipes you love and let it form the basis for a healthier you, a healthier family. The lifestyle you develop may very well save you from the ravaging effects of diabetes or heart disease. Each healthy step you take is cemented into a healthier body and an invitation to continue on the journey to a stronger version of *you*.

Spend some time reviewing the glossary. This is the overflow of extra wisdom you can cull as you go from your first taste of aquaponics to the advanced status of master gardener. You may have skimmed over much of the glossary at the beginning, wanting to digest each chapter as you flipped through the pages. That's okay. Just don't settle for a little knowledge. Understanding the underlying concepts is just as important as the initial reading.

And finish by going through the pictures again. One of those pictures resonated with you. It was a system you wanted the most. Look at it, and use it as your wish list for a garden of your own, a year round garden that never dies with winter's hoary breath. Pictures stimulate our hearts and minds, and I've given you many to salivate over.

I'm proud of you for sticking with it and reading the whole book. You have learned so much. Your family and friends will be thrilled with the outcome, and most importantly, so will you. Achievement is the highest form of growing self-reliance and self-confidence. Your knowledge and experience make you the expert everyone will turn to when they want to replicate your aquaponic garden. You're a rock star! Join some online groups and share what you know. The new friends you'll make will be people just like you. They're waiting for you!

HYDROPONICS

A Beginner's Guide to Building Your Own Hydroponic Garden

By Tom Gordon

HYDROPONICS

© Copyright 2019 - All rights reserved.

The content contained within this book may not be reproduced, duplicated or transmitted without direct written permission from the author or the publisher.

Under no circumstances will any blame or legal responsibility be held against the publisher, or author, for any damages, reparation, or monetary loss due to the information contained within this book. Either directly or indirectly.

Legal Notice:

This book is copyright protected. This book is only for personal use. You cannot amend, distribute, sell, use, quote or paraphrase any part, or the content within this book, without the consent of the author or publisher.

Disclaimer Notice:

Please note the information contained within this document is for educational and entertainment purposes only. All effort has been executed to present accurate, up to date, and reliable, complete information. No warranties of any kind are declared or implied. Readers acknowledge that the author is not engaging in the rendering of legal, financial, medical or professional advice. The content within this book has been derived from various sources. Please consult a licensed professional before attempting any techniques outlined in this book.

By reading this document, the reader agrees that under no circumstances is the author responsible for any losses, direct or indirect, which are incurred as a result of the use of information contained within this document, including, but not limited to, — errors, omissions, or inaccuracies.

INTRODUCTION

When we think of gardening, what we often see in our heads is a man or a woman on all fours crouched over a plot of dirt. They dig a hole, place in a seed or even a whole plant which they have bought, close it up and there you go. Or maybe we think of gardening in line with farming and we picture the same thing, only this time there isn't someone crouched down but a series of mechanical inventions that do all that busy work for them. We almost certainly don't think of an indoor setup, as that is more in line with hanging plants and decorative greens than it is with the concept of gardening. This would suggest that our main identifier which separates gardening from owning a few plants is the dirt itself, the soil which is part of Mother Earth. But the facts are quite different.

There are many different ways of gardening. The classic flowerbed in the front yard is just one of them. Here we'll be looking at another of them: Hydroponics. To say hydroponics is a new fad in the gardening world would discredit its history which reaches all the way back to the hanging gardens of Babylon and the Aztecs' floating gardens. There are even Egyptian hieroglyphs which describe a form of hydroponic. More recently, hydroponics was even given a place within NASA's space program. Clearly, this is not a new fad. But commercial growers and scientists are coming around to the method, leading to more hydroponic setups being used and more research looking into the advantages of hydroponics.

So, what makes hydroponic gardening different than traditional gardening? As the name implies (hydro) water plays a key role. The hydroponic garden actually doesn't make use of soil. Instead, hydroponic gardens make use of nutrient-based solutions through the circulation of water. So, a hydroponic garden tosses out the soil and instead uses an inert grow medium like clay pellets, vermiculite, perlite or one of several others that will pop up throughout this book. What this does is let the roots of the plant directly touch the nutrient solution, get more oxygen as they're not buried in the ground, and together these both promote growth.

The growth that this promotes can be quite astounding. A hydroponic setup, if managed properly, can actually see your plants maturing up to 25% faster than in typical soil gardening. Not only that but those plants that grow 25% faster might also yield up to 30% more as well! This is because the plants don't need to work as hard to get nutrients in a hydroponic setup as they would in a more traditional one. Basically, with the roots getting everything they need to provide the plant with nutrients, the plant can focus on growing its top part rather than having to grow out its roots for sustenance.

HYDROPONICS

But there are even more benefits to using a hydroponic setup than just expedient plant development. Despite the fact that hydro is in the name, hydroponic gardens actually use up less water than traditional soil-based gardens do. This is because the hydroponic system is an enclosed system. This means that there is less soil runoff, evaporation or wastewater in a hydroponic setup. Therefore, a hydroponic garden, when properly set up and maintained, will produce bigger plants at a faster rate with less environmental strain. It seems win-win-win, all around.

However, there are some slight disadvantages to hydroponic gardens over traditional soil-based gardens. The biggest and most obvious of these disadvantages is that a hydroponic garden will cost more to set up than a soil garden, regardless of size. With a soil garden, all you have to do is dig a hole, put in the plant or seed and then water it from time to time. This doesn't mean that you will have a healthy and well-functioning garden but it is pretty easy to get going. A hydroponic garden requires time and money to set up, especially if you've never set one up before. Plus, if you don't manage your hydroponic setup then it isn't very likely that it will keep those plants alive. Maintenance is super important here, that's why there's a whole chapter devoted to it later on. There are many different kinds of hydroponic gardens we can set up and some actually have more risks than others. For example, a setup that uses a pump (such as an ebb & flow system) can see that pump clog if not cared for properly and a clogged pump could see all your plants dead as result.

It should be noted that we are focused on hydroponic gardening which, despite the similarity in name, is not the same as aquaponic gardening. Aquaponic gardening is, in fact, a mixture of hydroponics with the growing and raising of fish. Basically, aquaponics is a hydroponic garden setup in which fish are introduced into the system. These fish create waste in the water which helps to give nutrients to the plants. The vegetables in the aquaponic garden, in return, clean the water for the fish. In this way, the aquaponic garden provides for both the fish that are being raised and the plants that are being grown. Aquaponic gardening is a great way of growing and raising food with an eye to sustainability. However, aquaponics gardening is beyond the scope of this specific book.

In this tome we will first explore the different types of hydroponic gardens we can set up. These will range from drip systems to ebb and flow systems, from aeroponics to wicking systems. We'll explore the advantages and disadvantages that they offer so that you have the knowledge you need to choose the type of system that works best for you. From there we will look into how these systems are built. While we won't be building every single kind of system that exists, we'll look at the general equipment that we need and explore the specifics of the most popular styles.

After we have our systems built, we'll talk about the operation cycle of hydroponic gardens. This means we'll explore how we set up our grow material, get seeds planted and discuss the different issues related to the lighting and trimming of our plants. Once we understand how to operate these systems, we'll take some time to examine the various plants that work best for hydroponic growth. We will also shed light on nutrition to figure out what exactly we mean when we use that word and what nutrients we feed into our systems.

With an understanding of the operation and nutrition of our hydroponic gardens, we will be able to move into a discussion on maintenance. This is one of the key areas that we need to grasp if we want to find success with our hydroponic gardens. Without proper maintenance, we can't expect to grow anything properly when we're fighting against clogs and bad pH levels. We'll move from maintenance into pests, which require another form of maintenance themselves. Thankfully, as we'll see, pests aren't nearly as common in a hydroponic setup as they are in traditional gardens. Finally, we will explore mistakes and myths that commonly pop up in regards to starting and maintaining a hydroponic garden.

HYDROPONICS

While these gardens do take more time to set up than the traditional, the knowledge in this book will give you a leg up in starting your own. But the benefits of hydroponic gardening speak for themselves: bigger plants in less time. Who wouldn't want that?

CHAPTER ONE

DIFFERENT TYPES OF HYDROPONIC GARDENS

If we want to become hydroponic gardeners, the first thing we need to do is understand what options are available to us. This way we can choose a method that has advantages and disadvantages that are properly in line with what we are looking for. This means, for example, if we don't want to risk clogs, we could avoid using methods that involve pumps. However, if we live in an area where we have a hard time controlling the amount of light in our environment, we might find ourselves looking to a system that uses a pump rather than one of the simpler ones like a deep-water culture in which light regulation is also important.

Each of these systems offers unique advantages and disadvantages from which we can choose. But this does not mean that one particular system is better than another. Like most things in life, the choice of which hydroponic system to use should be based on your

HYDROPONICS

schedule, needs and abilities. For this reason, I won't be extolling the virtues of any one particular system. Instead, we will look at the most popular systems around to see what their benefits are and what their disadvantages are. This way, you will have the knowledge necessary to choose the type that is right for you.

Hydroponic system

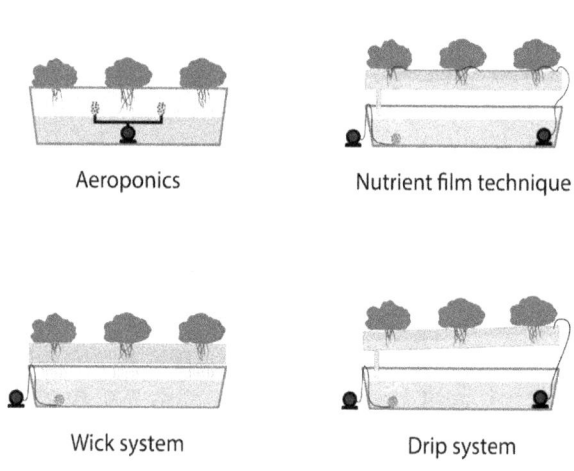

Aeroponics

Nutrient film technique

Wick system

Drip system

Drip System

This system is one of the most popular hydroponic setups but it was actually invented for outdoor gardens in Israel. At its most simplified, the drip system uses a pump to keep a drip of nutrient-rich water feeding our plants. The slow drip, rather than the typical spraying of water we see in gardens, allows for less water to be used.

Typically, a drip system is designed with two key parts. The first is the reservoir of nutrient-rich water that will feed the plants. Above this rests the grow tray in which our plants are potted. A pump is set up in the water and is connected up into the grow tray. From there, each of the plants will be given their own drip line. This means if you are growing four plants in your tray, you would use four drip lines. Sixteen plants, sixteen drip lines. However, because we want to give the growing medium, that substance you use to replace soil (and which we'll be looking at more in chapter three), time to breathe so as not to drown the plants, these drips will use a timer system. The growing medium will slowly release the water back down into the reservoir, creating a closed system.

A drip system offers us great control over the amount of water and nutrients that our plants are getting. With this system we are able to control the drip both by quantity and by length. This means if we use too much water in our drip, we can dial it back; or, if our drip is going too long or too short, we can adjust the timers that we are using to experiment until we find the length that's just right. One of the cool things about the drip system is that while it may take a while to set up and get right in the early period, once we have everything in place and know our volumes, the system doesn't require as much overall maintenance (depending on the particular setup) as other methods will. Plus, the materials needed to create a drip system aren't as costly as some of the others.

However, a drip system still uses a pump and a clogged pump can see our gardens decimated in merely a few hours. Of course, this depends on the size of the system. While the drip system is great for large-scale grow operations, it might be too complex for smaller operations. Some drip systems use what is called a non-recovery system which means that the water is not circulated back into the reservoir. These particular systems require less maintenance than systems which do feedback into the reservoir but in doing so they create more waste. This means that regardless of the system we use, we either will require more maintenance or create more waste.

A drip system works well for a variety of herbs and plants ranging from lettuce, onions, and peas to radishes, cucumbers, strawberries and pumpkins. It turns out that these systems actually are fantastic for larger plants. They also work best when making use of a growing medium in which water drains slowly like peat moss or coconut coir.

So, if you are looking to grow larger plants, the drip system is a great choice. Drip systems do require a bit of maintenance and they can be slow to set up at first but once they get going, they offer a high level of control over the growing process that any gardener would love.

Deep Water Culture

Considered the easiest of the hydroponic systems, a deep-water culture uses a reservoir system that the roots of the plants are suspended into. Basically, the plants sit above and instead of dripping water, they just reach down to take the water they want. This makes the system quite easy to set up.

A deep-water culture gets its name from the use of a deep reservoir and from how deep the roots go into the water. Other systems, such as the nutrient film technique, expose the roots of the plants to the air so that they can absorb plenty of oxygen. With this system we set up a grow tray above our reservoir, making sure that the material we use stops light getting through the system to prevent algae from growing inside and messing up the system. From there, the roots are suspended in the water and the water itself is kept oxygenated through the use of an air pump. This is done to keep the roots from drowning in the water.

HYDROPONICS

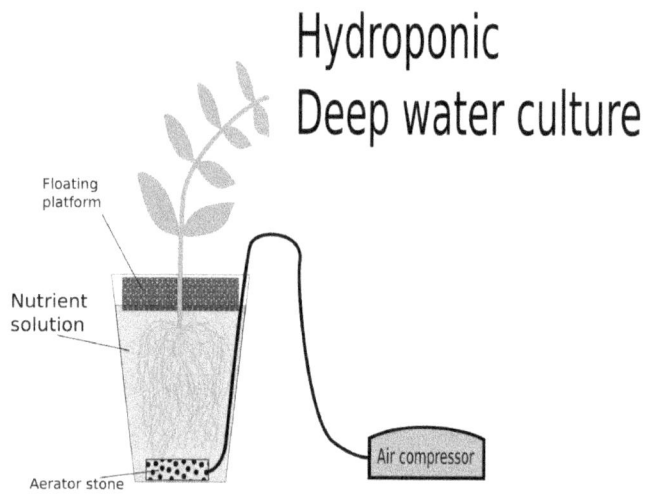

That's pretty much it. It wasn't a joke to say this is among the easiest of the hydroponic setups to get started with.

Deep water cultures are great for this simplicity but it is far from the only benefit that they offer. Because there are so few moving parts in a deep-water culture, they are rather low maintenance. There is an air pump but we don't pump water in this system and so the fear of losing our gardens to a faulty pump is unwarranted here. The easy setup and lower maintenance of these systems make them great for people first getting into hydroponic gardening and wanting to see if the approach is right for them.

However, while the deep-water culture's pump is air-based and so results in fewer blockages, they are still put at risk by power outages. Because the air pump is needed to oxygenate the water, a power outage could see your garden drown. Depending on the size of the system, it can be really tough to maintain proper pH levels in the water. A smaller system is harder to make minor changes in pH level to, as going just a little over or under can make a massive difference at smaller sizes. Finally, it can be really hard to keep a balanced water temperature in these systems as we have to be careful about the exposure of the reservoir to light.

Because of the way the system is set up, with the plants resting above the reservoir, the suitability of crops for the deep-water culture depends on several key factors. The first key is weight. If the plants we choose are too top-heavy, they can risk toppling over and breaking or even causing the weight of the setup to shift and knocking the top off. That's a disaster nobody wants to experience. The other major point is that we need to choose plants that like water. This means that plants which prefer dry growing conditions won't do very well in a deep-water culture. However, plants such as lettuce which love to soak up water will love this system.

Besides lettuce, some great choices for this system are herbs like basil and greens like kale, collard greens, chard and sorrel. Bok choy and okra also grow well in these systems and offer a variety outside of the traditional vegetables one thinks of as garden veggies.

So if you're looking to grow some water-loving plants, deep water culture is a system that is easy to set up and requires little maintenance. However, we have to be careful which plants we pick. If they are too top-heavy or prefer dry conditions, the deep-water reservoir isn't for them.

Nutrient Film Technique

With the nutrient film technique, we again use a reservoir of water but this time we are pumping it into a grow tray that has been set up at a slight angle. Doing it this way means that gravity takes care of getting the nutrient-rich water from one end of the tray to the other, where it will then drain back into the reservoir. More information about how we add nutrients to our water is covered in chapter four. Because of the design, this system is best used for plants with a smaller root system. The NFT setup is an active system.

The plants in the NFT system only have the ends of their roots touching the water, so as to keep the roots able to take in precious oxygen which helps growth. Because the system only uses a little water at a time, the plants are never drowned in the water.

HYDROPONICS

Because of the way the plants are positioned, it is very easy to check the roots for disease in the NFT system. The use of a reservoir of water that feeds back into itself reduces the overall waste of water and the design of the system makes it easy to scale the project up or down depending on the size needed. Plus, unlike deep water cultures, it can be fairly easy to get the pH levels right using an NFT setup.

However, the NFT also relies on a pump and so the risk of pump failure and the decimation of your crop is still a possibility that one has to look out for. Because of the way the roots are slotted into the system, they can block up the flow of water. This is why plants with a large root system like carrots aren't a good fit for the NFT system.

Because the roots are not actually in a growing medium like the other systems we looked at, this means that top-heavy plants don't work here either. However, leafy greens like lettuce or fruits like strawberries have found great success growing through an NFT system.

Ebb and Flow

The ebb and flow system get its name from the periodic flooding and draining of nutrient-rich water. It is also known, fittingly, as the flood and drain system. In this system, water floods into the glow tray and soaks the roots of the plants. Then the water drains back down into the reservoir. Flood, drain. Flood, drain. Over and over again, hence the name.

In order to get the system to work properly, we need to set up a pump to flood the grow tray. We set this pump up on a timer rather than let it constantly flood the grow tray and drown the plants. An overflow tube is set up in the grow tray so that the water drains back down into the reservoir. Depending on how we set it up, we might even include an air pump to make sure that the roots are getting the oxygen that they need.

The nice thing about the ebb and flow system is that it doesn't cost a lot to get started, as the materials aren't particularly hard to get a hold of. This system makes sure our plants are getting enough nutrients without drowning due to the easy to build structure. Once the system is set up, the hardest part of running it is out of the way. The ebb and flow system is able to run by itself once set up but you should still do maintenance to ensure everything is working properly.

Again, this system uses a pump, which means it can break and broken pumps are notorious for killing off entire gardens. If the structure fails to drain properly, the plants risk drowning and the pH levels in a broken system can be harmful to the plants. This is important to know because this system is prone to breakdowns and so we have to understand which areas a breakdown affects most.

One of the coolest things about the ebb and flow system is that it can be set up to allow just about any kind of plant or vegetable. Not so much the plants that prefer a dry system but size is not a concern here the way that it was in the nutrient film technique setup. Because of how easy it is to build the structure; we can alter it to fit the needs of our plants rather easily.

Wicking

Out of all of the systems we have and will look at, wicking is the easiest. It is so easy, in fact, that it is often recommended as an entry point to hydroponic gardening. Wicking is a passive system with very few parts, there are no water pumps in a wicked system.

In this system, we once again fill a reservoir with water and keep it beneath a grow tray. This time however, we don't use tubing to get the water to the plants but rather we set up a wicking material like rope. This wicking material is placed into the water and threaded up into the grow tray. Our grow tray is filled with a growing medium that is good at absorbing and keeping water because this system works very slowly. Water travels the length of the wick to slowly feed the plants.

HYDROPONICS

This system is great for its simplicity and can serve as an easy way to start getting into hydroponic gardening. It is also an inexpensive system, making it that much easier for the novice grower to invest in. Because there is no pump to break down, this system isn't at risk for premature death the way pump-based systems are. The lack of a pump also means that this system doesn't use up electricity and it can be refreshing to those worried about the size of their power bill.

However, despite its simplicity, there are still downsides to the wicking system that we have to consider. The system is inefficient at delivering nutrients, so plants that need a lot of water and nutrients aren't a very good match. The system can also see a toxic build-up of nutrients in the growing medium if we are not careful to observe how much water is getting in and being used.

Because of the lower water levels in wicking systems, they are best used for small plants. Lettuce and the smaller of the herbs make good fits for a wicking system but water-hungry plants like tomatoes would absolutely hate a wicking system. For this reason, the wicking system doesn't offer nearly the same variety as other systems. But that lack of variety is made up for by the ease of setup, making wicking a great system for those first trying their hands at hydroponics.

HYDROPONICS

Aeroponics

Saved the most complex for last. Aeroponics does away with the growing medium and instead leaves the roots of the plants exposed to more oxygen and so this system tends to see faster growth.

In this system, the roots of the plants hang down in the open air of the container in which the system is built. At the bottom of the system is our reservoir of nutrient-rich water. However, the roots don't dangle down into the water this time. Instead, we use a pump from the water to spray the plant roots with the nutrient solution. This pump is of course set up on a timer, to ensure we aren't overfeeding the plants. This makes it so that instead of the plant spending energy to grow out longer roots in search of nutrients, the nutrients come to the roots so that the plant can focus its growth elsewhere.

This system is great for producing larger plants since they don't need to focus on root growth. The lack of a growing medium also means that the roots don't need to take hold; we are bringing the nutrients directly onto them. The exposure of the roots to oxygen also helps to promote growth. This means that the aeroponic system is known for producing crops with impressive yields. This system also doesn't require a lot of space can so it can be built to be fairly mobile. Because of the lack of a growing medium, the aeroponic system is rather easy to clean.

We have to make sure to clean it because the constantly wet atmosphere of the system makes for an environment in which bacteria and fungi can thrive. The system is also very much prone to failures related to pumps and loss of power, which we've seen can be a major killer of our hydroponic gardens. The setup of an aeroponic garden also costs more than the other systems and it is the most technical of the hydroponic systems, which means the knowledge to entry is much higher as well. They also require constant supervision to protect against root diseases, fungi and to monitor pH levels and the density of the nutrient solution.

However, this system allows for bigger yields and the system can be used to grow almost any kind of plant. This means that the variety the aeroponic system offers is unparalleled compared to the other systems we have looked at.

Choosing the System That is Right for You

Like many things in life, the choice of which hydroponic system to use is a highly personal one. Each of us is after different goals with our gardens and has different skill levels when it comes to handling the technical stuff. This means that the best option available to us in order to figure out which system to use is to ask questions based around our needs and desires, such as:

HYDROPONICS

What is your skill level in putting together handy projects? If low, perhaps beginning with a wicking system would be an ideal start. What kinds of plants do you want to grow? If you are looking for top-heavy and larger plants, you are going to need to use a system that can support them. If you are looking for something smaller, you'll have more options but that doesn't mean you should go small if what you are after is a bigger plant. Do you have the time to invest in one of the more maintenance-heavy setups or would a more streamlined one like wicking fit into your life and gardening goals better?

HYDROPONICS

No Soil

Lorem ipsum dolor sit amet, consectetur adipiscing elit, sed do eiusmod tempor.

Fast Growth

Lorem ipsum dolor sit amet, consectetur adipiscing elit, sed do eiusmod tempor.

Less diseases

Lorem ipsum dolor sit amet, consectetur adipiscing elit, sed do eiusmod tempor.

Less pesticide use

Lorem ipsum dolor sit amet, consectetur adipiscing elit, sed do eiusmod tempor.

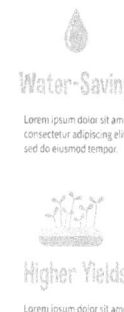

Water-Saving

Lorem ipsum dolor sit amet, consectetur adipiscing elit, sed do eiusmod tempor.

Higher Yields

Lorem ipsum dolor sit amet, consectetur adipiscing elit, sed do eiusmod tempor.

Affordable

Lorem ipsum dolor sit amet, consectetur adipiscing elit, sed do eiusmod tempor.

Each of the setups that we have explored in this chapter has been written about and explored in depth throughout the internet with many first-hand accounts of how they turned out. If one strikes you as intriguing, there is always more research that can be done to make sure that it is right for you. But one thing that stands out when you research these is that each one has been used

HYDROPONICS

successfully and has been demonstrated to have grown some amazingly healthy- and good-looking plants.

You know what you desire more than anyone else. Looking at the benefits, the plant types and the cons should give you a good idea of where to start. I suggest narrowing down to the couple that interest you most and going from there.

HYDROPONICS

Chapter Summary

- There are six main systems when it comes to hydroponic gardens.

- The drip system is designed to offer a timer-based drip onto each individual plant. It gives great control over how much water and nutrients our plants get and can be used to grow an impressive variety of plants.

- The deep-water culture is one of the easiest hydroponic setups; it allows the roots of the plant to be submerged in a nutrient solution.

- The nutrient film technique uses gravity and a water pump to soak the roots of our plants while also giving them plenty of exposure to air. NFT setups don't do well with large rooted plants or overly top-heavy ones.

- The ebb and flow systems work by flooding the plants and then draining out the water. This system can work with just about any kind of plant, giving it a lot of versatility.

- Wicking is the easiest of the hydroponic systems and takes its name from how it uses a fabric wick to transport water from the reservoir into our grow tray. This system is a great starter but it doesn't offer a ton of variety in what grows best.

HYDROPONICS

- Aeroponics is a hydroponic system which relies on misting the roots of the plants. It is the most technical of the systems to set up but can be the most rewarding. It also works with a wide array of plants.

- The system that works best for you is a personal choice depending on what you desire to grow and how much time and skill you have for setting up and maintaining your system.

In the next chapter, you will learn how to build your own hydroponic garden. We will look at how to set up a drip system, a wicking system and a deep-water culture. These range from beginner to intermediate in terms of difficulty setting up and so should make great entry points to those tackling hydroponic gardening for the first time.

CHAPTER TWO

HOW TO BUILD YOUR OWN SYSTEM

Now that we know the different kinds of hydroponic setups that are available to us, it is time to see how they are built. We will be looking at three of the different setups, those most suited for beginners. As we saw previously, each system has its own pros and cons. This means that the system you choose should be the one that fits your desires. However, this chapter can also help you to determine which setup is right for you based on how difficult it is to get it running.

While there are many sites and businesses out there that will sell you hydroponic kits, it can be very easy to make them ourselves. This isn't to say there is no value in store-bought kits. But before we go spending a lot of money, a DIY setup can be a great way to get a handle on the basics of setting up a hydroponic garden. Once we know what we are doing, we can then start to add on all sorts of gears and gizmos to personalize and level up our gardens. But we have to start somewhere and DIY is a great place to kick off from.

Drip System

For this system, we're going to look at one of the easy-to-build drip systems. This one uses buckets in which to grow the plants which still receive their nutrient-rich water through a series of tubes. In order to accomplish this design, there are three key areas which we need to build: the buckets, the reservoir and the tubing. We will look at what it takes to make a single plant setup but we'll see how easy it is to adapt the system to include more.

Start with your bucket. For our purposes, we'll begin with a five-gallon bucket but you can increase or decrease the size as necessary. The first thing we do is flip the bucket upside down so that we can get at the bottom easily. We're looking to get the drain into place so that any water dripped into the system will be recycled back into the reservoir. To do this we will be using a thru-hole fitting. These little guys are used in all sorts of different fields and you can easily pick one up for a dollar or two at any hardware store.

Place the thru hole on the bottom of the bucket, thread side making contact, and trace around it. This should give you a small little circle on the bottom of your

HYDROPONICS

buckets. We want this circle to be closer to the edge than to the middle, as we want our bucket to be able to sit comfortably on an elevated surface. With that in place, cut out the circle you have traced and insert the thru hole into the bucket. Tighten the thru hole in place. Your bucket now has a drain installed. Take a filter of some sort, can be a furnace filter or any kind really, and cut enough out to place over the thru hole inside the bucket. This helps to keep only water draining and not our growing medium.

Now before we move onto the next step, we should paint our buckets. We can double up this task and paint our reservoirs at the same time. Use a black paint on the outside of the bucket in order to block light from entering which would lead to algae growth. With the buckets painted black, they are going to attract a lot of heat which would raise the temperature of our water and could prove to be a real pain in the long run. For this reason, it is suggested that you use a coat or two of white paint over the black paint so as to reflect the light rather than absorb it.

We're going to do a similar design when it comes to our reservoir but the key difference is the hole we cut will be in the top and not in the bottom. Having painted the reservoir black and then white, we will cut a hole in the top of it through which we can feed the cording for our pump and for the hoses. That's all that the reservoir takes.

HYDROPONICS

But in order to make this work from here, we need to connect them using tubing. Connect the tube to the hose and feed it up to the bucket. You can use glue, tape, or whatever method you prefer in order to keep the tube in place to feed your plants. One effective way is to create a loop that sits inside the inside of the bucket, poke a ton of little holes in it and then connect that tube to your main tube. That way water would flow up through the main tube, connect to the inner bucket tube and it would work like a mini sprinkler system. This way makes sure that the water is spread around the bucket and not confined to a single area.

With the feeder tube in place, we then need to attach the draining tube. This is as easy as hooking our tubing up to the thru hole we inserted and running it back down into the reservoir. It is important that we keep our grow bucket elevated above the reservoir so that gravity can do its trick.

In order to make sure that we aren't drowning our plants, it's important that we get a digital timer and hook it up so that we aren't pumping water at all times. We'll want to get a timer that allows us to set many different times rather than just one time because we want our system to turn off and on several times a day rather than just once. We need to do this in order to make sure that our plants are getting the right amount of nutrients.

HYDROPONICS

So that is how you set up a single bucket drip system. If you want to expand the system, it is actually very easy. Let's say that you wanted to do four buckets instead of just one. You take those buckets and you give them their thru holes and a paint job all the same. The major difference between running a single bucket setup and a four bucket setup is the tubing. Rather than running a single tube from our reservoir to our bucket, we are going to instead use T-connectors.

Take the tubing that runs out of the reservoir and connect it into a T-connector. This will give you a tube that looks like a T-corner like we see on the roads. Instead of being a single tube with one ending, you now have two tubes each with their own ending. This would allow us to use a two bucket setup. However, we choose a four bucket setup for this example. This means that we have to take each of those tubes and again run them into a T-connector. Now each side gets split into two and we have four ends, one for each of our buckets and we have quadrupled the size of our grow operation.

With all the building in place, we then just have to pack in our buckets. Some rocks at the bottom of each bucket can serve to help weigh them down but it's not absolutely needed. This is more a precaution, though it is one that is recommended. Over the rocks, you pack in your growing medium and then you get your plants in there.

HYDROPONICS

And there you have it, your very own hydroponic drip system.

Wicking System

As we saw above, wicking is actually the easiest of the systems to get started with. It's also one of the easiest systems to build as it requires very little technical skill. All we need to get started is a growing tray, a reservoir and a material for wicking.

Wicking is simply the use of a wickable material going from our reservoir to our grow tray. This can be rope, felt, string; whatever material you can easily get your hands on for the wicking will work.

We will first set up our reservoir, filling it with our nutrient solution of choice, which of course depends on what we are growing (for more information on nutrient solutions, see chapter four). Again, we are going to paint the reservoir black and then cover it in a coat of white paint to prevent it from supporting algae or growing too hot. We are then going to cut or drill very small holes in the cover of the reservoir through which we will thread our wicks.

Our grow trays are going to be filled with a medium that is particularly well-suited to wicking such as perlite or coco coir. But before we fill them up, we first want to cut or drill tiny holes into the bottom of the tray as we did to the cover of the reservoir. These will be roughly the same size because they are how the wick gets the nutrients to the plants.

Ultimately, we have our wicks almost entirely submerged in the water. This doesn't necessarily mean that they are touching the bottom of the reservoir but they are certainly coming close. They are then fed up and nested in the growing tray very close to the plants. We can use more than one wick per plant depending on the plant's particular water and nutrient needs.

As far as set up, that's really it. We place our plants into the grow tray and we watch how they grow. However, there are some tips and tricks that will make a more successful wicking system. We might consider using an air pump to aerate the water so that our plants are able to get more oxygen as this will help them to grow faster. Another thing we will want to consider is keeping the grow tray closer to the reservoir with a wicking system than we would with a drip system. This is because the nutrients aren't pumped to our plants in this system but have to rely on what is called capillary action (aka, wicking). Having our wicks shorter means, they can more easily provide. The distance between our wicks and the grow tray is one way of doing this. Another is making sure that the level of the water in our reservoir is high, as this shortens the distance as well.

Again, this system isn't great for plants that require a lot of water and nutrients because the wicking of nutrients is a slow process. However, herbs and lettuce can grow great crops in a wicking system and this makes for an easy way to introduce the concepts of hydroponics to someone new to the topic. They even make great projects for getting kids into hydroponics and gardening!

Deep Water Culture

Despite the wicking system being considered the easiest of the hydroponic systems to get started gardening with, the deep-water culture is just about as easy when it comes to building. For our purposes of explanation, we will be making a single deep-water culture. This means that we will be designing one as if we were growing a single medium-size plant. This system can be adapted to fit multiple smaller plants, though if we want to go bigger, we will have to change our culture to a larger container first.

Since a deep-water culture uses deep water (it's there in the name, after all), we will be using a five-gallon bucket because of the depth that it gives us. While some people refer to any system of plants floating on the water as a deep-water system, we actually need to have ten plus inches of water for it to be considered deep. We could grow a small plant in a small culture and have it be equivalent in ratios to that of a deep water culture but it still wouldn't be proper to call it such.

The first thing that we are going to do, surprise, is paint our bucket black and then white. Slightly underneath the lid, we are also going to cut a little hole for the tubing of our air pump so that we can oxygenate the water. With these two steps out of the way, we can set our buckets to the side.

Because a deep-water culture works by having the roots of the plant soaking in the water, we need to design a setup so that our plants can bath. To do this, we can go out and buy what is called a plant basket. This is a basket that looks like your typical plant pot but instead, it has a ton of holes through the lower half. Alternatively, we can also just take a plant pot and then cut, drill or solder holes into it. This is going to be our grow tray.

We'll be filling our grow tray up with our desired growing medium and the plant that we want to raise but first, we need to integrate it into the system. To do this we will be cutting a hole in the lid of our five-gallon bucket. At this point, it is best to cut a smaller hole and make it larger as needed rather than start with a large hole. This is because it is far easier to increase the size of the hole than it is to block it back up. If we make our hole too big, our grow tray will just fall into the bucket and we will need to get another lid and try all over again. Our goal is for the lower half of the pot to fit into the hole and be held in place by the pot's rim against the bucket's lid.

Earlier, we cut a hole in our bucket just under the lid for our air pump. The reason we didn't cut it on the lid itself is that when we open our system up to check the pH levels and make sure our nutrients are all balanced, we don't want to have to fiddle around with any wires. When we open our system, we should only have to remove the lid and thus the plant pot.

Everything should now be in place. We're going to fill up the bucket with our water, bringing it up to cover three-quarters of the plant pot that is hanging down inside it. We might want to test this first with plain water so that we can then mark the desired water level on our buckets to make it easier to see going forward. Mix together your nutrient solution, fill the plant potter with your desired growing medium and add your plant or seed.

It will take a week or so for the roots of the plant to start poking out of the holes that we drilled into our pot, so it is important to make sure that the water level is high enough for our plants to get the moisture they need. As the roots begin to hang down, the water level won't matter nearly as much.

And there you have it, you just created a deep-water culture for your plants. While you can grow a medium-sized plant or a couple of small ones in this one culture, you are most likely going to want to set up a couple. But as you've seen, that shouldn't take very much time at all.

HYDROPONICS

Chapter Summary

- Building a drip system requires tubing, a reservoir, a bucket and a pump. This system requires a little bit of work but is very easy to scale to the size you require.

- In order to prevent algae from growing in our reservoirs, we paint them black. In order to prevent them from absorbing too much heat, we cover the black paint with white paint.

- All we need to set up a wicking system is to drill a hole through the top of our reservoir and the bottom of our growth tray and thread through a wickable material. This makes wicking the easiest of all the systems and great for beginners.

- A deep-water culture involves setting up a deep bucket or container of water and then hanging our growing pots down into it. This easy-to-set-up system allows us to grow one medium-sized or a handful of smaller-sized plants. While not as scalable as the drip system, ease of setup makes it a great option.

In the next chapter, you will learn all about the operation cycle of hydroponic gardens. From the choice of growing medium to how we seed our plants and from lighting to trimming. While none of these steps are particularly difficult in and of themselves, we want to make sure that we have a strong grasp of each of them.

CHAPTER THREE

OPERATION CYCLE

Now that we have got a hydroponic system set up, let us take some time to look at how the operation works. This means that we will be exploring the different kinds of growing mediums available to us to see what works best for which kinds of setups. We will also explore how we seed our hydroponic gardens, how we light them and what we do when the time comes for trimming.

Growing Mediums

When it comes to what medium we use in our grow trays, there is a ton of variety available to us. This can be a little intimidating at first when you aren't sure which medium is right for you and the gardening that you are looking to do. It is important that we choose a medium that works with the plants we are planning to plant. This means that we have to take into account things like water retention and pH balance.

Before we look at the mediums themselves, a quick word on the requirements of the different systems. The way that each system is set up and works actually says a lot about what kind of growing medium works best. For example, a drip system functions best when it is using a growing medium that doesn't become too soggy. In contrast, a wick system likes a growing medium that absorbs and holds onto water and moisture with ease. While nutrient film technique systems want to avoid a growing medium that easily saturates, an ebb and flow system will want to have good drainage and a growing medium that doesn't float. Considering the mechanics of your system of choice is the first step in deciding a growing medium.

Coco Coir

An organic and inert grow medium, coco coir is made from the frayed and ground husks of coconuts. When it comes to pH, coco coir is very close to neutral. Coco coir retains water but also allows a decent amount of oxygen to get through which helps the roots. This medium is primarily used in container growing or in hydroponic systems of the passive variety such as wicking. Because it can clog up pumps and drippers, it is

HYDROPONICS

not a great choice for more active systems such as the ebb and flow system.

Gravel

Gravel doesn't absorb or retain moisture. Instead, gravel works to give an anchor for the roots of the plant. For this reason, gravel works best in a system which doesn't require a ton of retention such as a drip system or a nutrient film technique system. Any system that keeps the roots of the plant in constant contact with the water can make good use out of gravel.

In some setups, such as the bucket-based drip system we saw above, gravel is used as a bottom layer in the pot. This allows for better drainage as the water has passed through whatever medium made up the top layer to find gravel which doesn't retain it whatsoever. It also serves to add some weight to the bottom of your tray which can help to prevent spills from wind or other elements.

If you are using gravel, make sure to give it a proper wash before use in the system. If you want to reuse the gravel, make sure to wash it yet again. We do this to prevent salts or bacteria from getting into the hydroponic system and causing issues such as burnt roots, high levels of toxicity and the like. Jagged gravel can also damage the roots so it is best to use smooth gravel as a way of avoiding this.

Perlite

Perlite is actually an amendment to our growing mediums, which means that it is used to improve an existing medium rather than just being used on its own. You make perlite by heating up glass or quartz sand, though of course we don't have to make it ourselves but can buy it from any gardening store. Perlite helps to improve the drainage and aeration when mixed in with another growing medium such as coco coir.

HYDROPONICS

Because we are using a nutrient mix and not just pure water, we have to be concerned about nutrient build-up. The nutrients in our solutions can get absorbed into the grow medium and lead to a build-up of toxicity which risks killing off our plants No gardener wants that. The extra drainage that perlite offers will help to prevent this build-up and will help in making sure that our plant's root system get the oxygen it needs to grow. Perlite comes in different grades from fine and medium through to coarse. The kind you need will be determined by the rest of your potting mix. Perlite should never take up more than a third of your mix, however, as using too much will cause it to float and floating perlite doesn't offer the benefits, we wanted it for in the first place.

HYDROPONICS

Vermiculite

Vermiculite is actually a lot like perlite. It comes in three different grades, again ranging from fine and medium through to coarse. Made by expanding mica through heat, vermiculite is another soil and potting mix amendment. This means that vermiculite is mixed with another growing medium in order to get the best results.

Vermiculite sort of works like the reverse perlite. Where perlite helped with the drainage of our growing medium, vermiculite helps our growing medium to retain water. For this reason, vermiculite can often be seen mixed with perlite for use in hydroponic systems of the passive variety such as wicking systems.

Rockwool

One of the most popular of the growing mediums, Rockwool is made through the heating and spinning of certain silica-based rock into a cotton candy-like material. This creates a firm material that tends to have the ideal ratio of water to oxygen that our plants' roots love. It also is mostly pH neutral, which is always a plus.

It can be found in a bunch of different shapes and sizes with the most common being a cube shape. These cubes are awesome for starting out seeds (which we'll look at more in just a moment). These smaller cubes are often used in order to begin the growing of a plant before being transferred into another growing medium.

Because of the versatility of Rockwool, it can be used for starting plants before transferring into another medium for deep water cultures or nutrient film technique systems. It can also be used for drip systems and ebb and flow systems without the need to transfer.

Mixing Your Growing Medium

When it comes to which growing medium is the best, it depends on the job that you are looking to have it tackle. Once you have an idea of what you need, you can begin the task of mixing it all together. There are many different projects on the market that offer premixed growing mediums and these can be a great way to save a little time and get what you need right out of the box.

However, some of us are a little more specific and we like to get our hands dirty in this part of the process. Mixing your own growing medium can be a great way to make sure it is 100% the way you want it to be. But this can be a little tricky if you are new to hydroponic gardening and don't know what combination of mediums is best. Part of getting into anything new, and hydroponic gardening is no different, is that you have to accept some uncomfortable moments and you have to accept that you will learn from your mistakes.

For an example of one mixture, let us look at what Upstartfarmers.com have laid out in their discussion on soilless potting. They offer a formula for a mixture that is one-part coconut coir or peat, one-part perlite or vermiculture and two parts compost. While the systems we have looked at aren't focused on compost but rather getting nutrients through our reservoir's solution, this shows us a straightforward mixture. Notice that the perlite or vermiculite does not exceed 33% (or 1/3rd) of the total mixture.

HYDROPONICS

Seeding

When it comes to getting plants into our hydroponic system, we have two options available to us. We can go to the store and we can purchase a seedling which we then transplant into our system. Or we can purchase seeds and we can raise the plants ourselves. In this section, we will be looking at this second option to see how it is we can turn seeds into wonderful plants for our hydroponic gardens. But this means that we will also be exploring the first option because when our seeds are ready to be moved into our hydroponic setups, we will be transplanting them as seedlings.

There is a lot of satisfaction to be found in growing a plant out of a seed. They start out as tiny grains and yet can grow to be such big and luscious plants. It really is a wonderful feeling to know that you are the one responsible for making that come to pass. But there are benefits to growing from seed beyond just the feeling that it gives us.

When you purchase seeds, you are getting many chances at growing the plants you want. Not every seed will take but enough of them will that you can easily get a ton more plants through seeds for the same price that you would go out and get a single seedling. This makes it a cost-effective approach, as well as one that just feels really awesome. Purchasing seeds also gives you more control over what you grow, as you are not limited in

HYDROPONICS

options to only the seedlings that the store had available when you went looking. This means that you can be the one to choose what you grow and it could be rare and esoteric plants or just some lettuce and herbs. The choice is up to you.

If you grow the seeds directly in the hydroponic system which you are planning to use, then you don't have to worry about transplanting your greens into a new system. This can be a way to avoid causing the plants trauma or ending up with root damage. Transplanting into the system can also be a way to introduce disease or pests into your garden and we want to avoid this whenever possible.

HYDROPONICS

When we decide that we are going to start with seeds, it does cost us a little bit of money upfront because we need to create a few things for them to start to grow. However, this cost is mostly when just beginning. If you have already started with seeds before, you can expect to save some money when you come to them next. The good news is that you really don't need to go out of your way to buy super specialized equipment or materials to begin growing from seeds. All of the materials that you pick up can have uses at other steps in the process.

Assuming that you have already gone and picked out some seeds, what do you need to get them started in your hydroponic garden? The first thing we need is a grow tray. This can be one that we have set up before, or we can make one with a dome shape to it so as to create a miniature greenhouse. Don't worry if you don't have one that fits that description, this is just one way to help our seeds out. We can use whatever grow tray we have available.

We want to make sure that we position our grow tray so that it gets good light - if the plants are the type that likes lots of light. We also want to make sure that the tray gets a good amount of heat. Getting a heating pad that goes under or making sure it is kept in a warm area will help to make sure that sprouting begins to happen.

HYDROPONICS

At this stage, we have two options available to us. Our grow tray can be used specifically just for these seeds, which would mean that we have to transplant them when they have grown into seedlings, or we can use a grow tray that is ultimately part of the hydroponic setup itself. Going the second route can be useful because it avoids the traumas that can happen when trying to transplant our seedlings.

After we have a tray set up, we are going to want to go out and get or make some starting plugs. These are little compact masses of solid growing medium that are used specifically for the growing of our seeds They tend to be made up of composted pine and peat or other organic matter. We can purchase them or make them, as they are basically little cubes of the material with a small hole for us to put our seeds into.

Open up your plug and drop a couple of seeds inside of it. We do a couple just in case any of the seeds don't want to take. If multiple take, we can always remove the weaker plant so that the stronger one can grow even better. After you have dropped your seeds into the hole, tear off a tiny piece of the plug and use it to block the hole. You do this to prevent your seeds from drying out or getting knocked out of the plug.

In the grow tray, you will need about an inch of nutrient solution, though you only want that inch to be at half the strength that it would normally be at. Place the seeded plugs into the tray. You can expect to start seeing some sprouts emerge within four or five days from planting. Make sure that you keep an eye on the water levels throughout this period and add more nutrient solution as the levels decrease.

That's how you grow from seed. Now, if you have set this up in your main grow tray, you don't have to worry about transplanting them later and you can just let them grow and continue watching them as you would any other plant in your garden. If you started them in a tray specifically for seeds, however, then you are going to need to transplant them into your system.

As your seedlings start to grow stronger, you can stop worrying about halving the strength of the nutrient solution and begin them on the regular strength solution mix. When you start to see the roots of the seedlings coming out of the bottom of the starter plug, this is the sign that you can now begin transplanting them. This could be anywhere from two to four weeks; it all depends on which plants you are growing.

Now that the seedlings are ready, you are going to take them and gently move them over to your hydroponic setup. To do this you are going to take the seedling and the cube together. You want to open up a spot in your garden, gently place the cube and seedling into said spot and then cover it gently with your growing medium of choice. After this is done, you will want to water the plant from the top for a few days so that it grows out its root system and naturally seeks out water and nutrients.

And that's it! Now you have grown your very own plant from seed through to seedling and all the way through transplanting and developing a root system naturally. Working with seeds this way allows us to take more control over what we grow and to make sure that we aren't introducing any problems into our garden that may be found in the seedlings available for purchase at the store.

Lighting

When it comes to lighting, there can be no substitute that makes up for the power of the sun. There is a reason that spring and summer are such beautiful, green times of the year. The sun is absolutely the most powerful lighting source available for plants.

But we're not going to be using it here, despite all that. Instead, we are going to be using artificial lighting so that we have complete control over it. Not only that, but many of us are interested in hydroponics because we don't have access to an outdoor space in which to garden. If you live in an apartment, chances are you're reading this because it offers you an option for growing your own food without having to leave home. If you can

HYDROPONICS

set up your hydroponic garden so that it takes advantage of natural sunlight, that's great! But if you can't, you need to look into artificial lighting and that's what we'll be exploring.

There are tons upon tons of options available for lighting. So many that it can be really overwhelming if you are new to the topic. What size light do you want? What color spectrum is it supposed to be playing within? Heck, how much light is the right amount? It can truly be daunting. But don't worry, it's a lot easier than all those choices make it out to seem.

Tackling the amount of light, we can use the sun as a basis for this. If we were growing plants outside, we can expect them to need about five hours of direct sunlight and another ten of indirect sunlight. This means five hours soaking in the sun and ten hours being outside but getting a little shade. Using this system, we can adjust our artificial lighting accordingly. Using artificial lights, we should be giving our hydroponic garden about fourteen hours of bright light and ten hours of darkness. Doing this system everyday imitates the sun's natural lighting cycle. Don't skimp on the darkness, either. You might think that more light means faster growth but plants are just like us in that they need to rest and metabolize the nutrients that they are getting.

Some plants need more light, some plants need less. You can think of the fourteen-ten system as a general.

HYDROPONICS

This system works well for most plants and can definitely be a successful route to take with your garden. But you should definitely be aware of the light requirements of your plants.

Some plants like short days, which means they want longer periods of darkness in which to function. With these plants, being exposed to more than twelve hours of light per day can actually cause them to not flower properly. Strawberries and cauliflower are examples of short-day plants. The short-day cycle actually works to imitate the shorter days of the spring in which these plants like to grow.

Long-day plants are those that want to get up to eighteen hours of sunlight per day. These ones are mimicking the longer day cycle that comes with the summer season. Examples of long-day plants include lettuce, potatoes, spinach and turnips. Because they like more light, you wouldn't want to mix long-day plants with short-day plants in the same growing tray. If you do, expect to pick a lighting cycle that meets in the middle of long and short needs.

There are also plants which are more neutral. These plants tend to be flexible and can work with more or less light as needed. Eggplant and corn are examples of these sorts of plants. Day-neutral plants can be mixed together with either short-day or long-day plants and grow equally well.

HYDROPONICS

Because you want to mimic the sun, the best option for lighting your hydroponic garden is to get a timer. If you set up an ebb and flow system earlier, you probably have already gotten yourself a timer to make sure that you are letting your nutrient solution drain before washing over them again. We basically use the same kind of timer, only instead of being set up to a pump, we have set it up to our lights. How long you set the timer for will depend on what you are growing and their light needs as discussed above.

When it comes to the lights themselves, we need to get into a discussion on bulbs. The most popular bulb to use in hydroponics tends to be between 400-600 watts and of a kind called High-Intensity Discharge. These bulbs tend to be encased in glass (with gas and metal salts thrown into the mix) and they create light through sending electricity between two electrodes within. The gas helps the bulb to create the arc and the metal salts evaporate to make white light. They come in two types: high-pressure sodium bulbs and metal halide bulbs.

The metal halide bulb works as an all-round light that most vegetables will love. If you have to choose between metal halide or high-pressure sodium bulbs, the metal halide is the better choice. They tend to be expensive, upwards of $150 for a 400-watt bulb but they only need to be replaced every other year, though they may decrease in efficiency earlier.

HYDROPONICS

High-pressure sodium bulbs are best used for the flowering stage of our plants. These are even more expensive than metal halide bulbs but they tend to last up to twice as long. However, they do also lose efficiency like the metal halide bulbs.

If we want to increase the efficiency of our bulbs, we can use a reflector hood. This is a reflective case that goes around the bulb and increases its effectiveness by bouncing the light around. This helps the light to hit our plants from different angles so that we can get a more effective spread onto our garden. It also serves to get a little more heat out of the bulbs, as the light beams are now crossing each other and make up a denser section and thus carry more heat and power.

So when it comes to lighting, if you can only get one bulb, go out and get yourself a metal halide bulb and a reflector hood. Get yourself a timer and make sure that you set it to the needs of your plants. When buying plants, you almost always will receive a tag with some information about the light requirements of the plant or the seeds. Following this and setting up an appropriate timer will make sure that your plants get all the light they need.

Trimming

HYDROPONICS

The final step in the operation cycle of our hydroponic gardens is trimming. When plants are out in the wild, nature plays the role of gardener and trimmer. These plants can go many years, sometimes even their whole life, without being trimmed or pruned. Once you bring your plants indoors, either inside with a hydroponic setup or in a greenhouse, people immediately start reaching for those pruning shears. When we consider the image of gardening we have in our heads, we can see that movies and TV have told us again and again that we want to prune our plants. Characters are always doing it!

But the truth is that if we don't prune our plants properly, we actually risk hurting them. To be clear, this means that the pruning we are doing is the thing that can hurt them. Not a lack of pruning. Improper pruning causes unneeded stress on our plants and can do some serious damage to them, even going so far as to leave them vulnerable to disease or infection. This is because each time we prune our plants, what we are doing is opening up a wound. We cut off a branch, we have just torn open our plants. Where there was a hand, figuratively, there is now just a stump. If you think about the human body, you can see why this could easily go wrong. We need to give our plants' bodies the same respect we would give another human's. This means that when you go to prune, make sure that you sterilize your cutting instrument between every cut. This can be done as simply as mixing four parts water with one-part bleach and dunking your shears into the solution before each cut.

So if pruning our plants can be so harmful, what are the reasons that we choose to do it? There are actually quite a few reasons. One is that we want to control the overall size of our plants. If we are growing inside, we may prune our plants to prevent them from reaching out and getting in the way of walking areas or the television, things like that. This is the same reason that we cut tree branches when they get too close to power lines. We might also cut our plants to improve their health and the quality of their flowering. If a particular piece of the plant is dead and rotting, we need to remove that piece

HYDROPONICS

to promote the plant's health. We may also want to remove bits that didn't flower properly, that way the healthy flowering parts have more room to breathe and space to expand. This will also stop the plant from spending energy trying to repair damaged parts and instead it can use that energy for growing.

One reason NOT to trim your plants is to increase the overall yield. Trimming doesn't help our plants in this way. Rather than trim to increase, we should be trimming to promote better health.

When we have decided where we plan to prune, we know we need a sterilizing solution for our shears. Another way to prevent diseases during the pruning process is to pinch the ends of the plant where you have made the cut. This will help to get the ends to heal together quicker. It's kind of like stitching up a cut on your arm. You want to keep the ends together so that healing is promoted and the time it takes to heal is reduced. Because pruning the plant is so stressful and healing takes energy, you should really only prune when absolutely necessary and you shouldn't just make cuts willy nilly. It might be best to prune a little, wait for the plant to heal and then prune some more rather than do it all in one big burst.

If the reason you are pruning your plant is that it is growing too high for the area you are housing it in, consider doing what is called "topping." When we prune in this manner, what we are doing is cutting off the top of the main stem of the plant. Once we make the cut, we are going to then pinch it together as we do with any of our cuts. However, pinching the top of the main stem after a cut gets the plant to release floral hormones which will cause the plant to begin focusing on growing sideways rather than upwards. This same technique can then be applied to these lateral branches to achieve a reverse effect where it begins to grow upwards again. In this way, topping allows us to get some control over the growing patterns of our plants. Topping also leads to a weird effect where gardeners have noticed that plants which have been topped tend to produce more small fruit. Meanwhile, plants that haven't been topped tend to produce less fruit but of a large size.

If you are pruning to remove damaged and dying leaves, you should only be removing leaves that are more than half damaged. These leaves are no longer providing the plant with energy and instead are actually draining it of some in its attempts to heal them. There is a misguided idea that if a plant's leaves turn yellow, you should immediately remove them. However, turning leaves yellow is actually the plant's way of trying to tell you that something is wrong. It typically means that the plant is undergoing a lot of stress. This could mean that it isn't getting the nutrients and light it needs or maybe it is even a sign that the plant is dealing with an insect problem. When your plant's leaves start turning yellow, you should look at what the plant is trying to tell you before you start to cut it. If you fix the problem, quite often you will see the leaves take on their healthier green color again.

So, when it comes time to start pruning your plants, make sure that you sterilize your instruments, think about how much stress you are putting on the plant and only make cuts that are absolutely necessary. We want to grow healthy and fruitful plants and this means respecting the bodies of your plants like you would respect your own.

HYDROPONICS

Chapter Summary

- There are many different growing mediums available to us on the market today. We can even mix together our own if we want.

- Coco Coir retains water but allows decent oxygen to get through. However, it is prone to clogging up pumps.

- Gravel doesn't retain moisture but serves to anchor our plants. It is also good for weighing down our grow trays so they don't accidentally spill.

- Perlite is best used in addition to another growing medium and helps to offer better drainage.

- Vermiculite is the reverse perlite; we add it to another growing medium in order to help with retaining moisture.

- Rockwool offers a lot of versatility as a growing medium and is great for starting out your seeds.

- Purchasing seeds tends to be better than buying seedlings as it gives us more chances to grow plants and a better control over what plants we want to grow.

HYDROPONICS

- We start our seeds out in starting plugs in a grow tray with a nutrient solution at half the strength of our regular system.

- Once the seeds begin to sprout, we transfer the seedling (starting plug and all) into our hydroponic setup.

- When it comes to lighting our hydroponic garden, we aim to recreate a light cycle similar to the sun. The plants we are growing will determine if we need more or less light hours than a typical day.

- Trimming our plants is actually a form of harming them and so we should only prune our plants when we absolutely have to.

- If we are pruning for size, we should be considering a topping method so that we can control how they grow out.

In the next chapter, you will learn all about the plants that work best in our hydroponic gardens. Not only that but we will take a look at the nutrients we are feeding them.

CHAPTER FOUR

BEST PLANTS FOR HYDROPONIC GARDENING AND NUTRITION

We know what each of the hydroponic garden setups are, how we make several of our own and what kind of operation cycle we can expect to be going through. In this chapter, we are going to take a look at the different plants that are available for us to grow. We will take a brief look at each plant to get an idea of how they best grow in our hydroponic setups. From there we will be looking at the nutrition that our plants require.

Vegetables

When it comes to vegetables, there are a ton of options available to us. We'll be looking at a handful of these but first, let's tackle some general rules of thumb.

First up are those vegetables that grow underneath the soil. These are vegetables like onions, carrots and potatoes. These plants can still be grown in a hydroponic system but they require extra work compared to those that grow above the surface like lettuce, cabbage and beans. This means that those under-the-soil plants require a little more advanced skill, and you may want to get some experience with your hydroponic system before you try to tackle them.

The other rule of thumb is that we should try to avoid crops like corn and zucchini and anything that relies on growing lots of vines. These types of plants take up a ton of space and just aren't very practical crops for hydroponic systems. Instead of focusing on a plant type that isn't practical, we can make better use of our space and systems.

Beans

There are many different types of beans from green beans to pole beans, lima beans to pinto beans. Depending on the type of bean you plant, you may want to consider adding a trellis to your setup. Beans offer a wide variety for what you can add them to and they make a great side dish to just about any meal. When it comes to temperature, beans prefer a warm area. They also prefer a pH level of around 6.0.

If you are growing your beans from seeds, you can expect them to take between three and eight days to germinate. From there you can expect another six to eight weeks before it is time to harvest. After harvesting begins, the crop can be continued for about another three or four months.

Cucumbers

Like beans, there are a few different options when it comes to what kind of cucumber we can grow. There are thick-skinned American slicers, smooth-skinned Lebanese cucumbers, seedless European cucumbers. So a wide variety, and the best news is they all grow pretty well in a hydroponic setup. Where beans prefer a warm temperature, cucumbers prefer straight-up hot. They like to be a step beyond just warm. They also prefer a pH level between 5.5 and 6.0

HYDROPONICS

It only takes between three and ten days for cucumbers to begin to germinate. They take between eight to ten weeks to get ready for harvesting. When it comes to harvesting cucumbers, make sure that the cucumbers have taken on a dark green color and that they are firm when you grasp them. Because each cucumber grows at a different rate, you can expect the harvesting to take some time as you don't want to pick them before they are ready.

Kale

Kale is a delicious and nutritious vegetable that makes a great addition to just about any meal. There are so many health benefits to kale that it is often considered a superfood. Kale actually prefers a slightly cooler temperature; it grows best in a range between cool to warm. Like cucumbers, kale prefers a 5.5 to 6.0 pH level.

Seed to germination only takes four to seven days. However, to get harvesting takes between nine and eleven weeks. It's a little bit longer to grow kale than either beans or cucumbers but you can harvest it in such a way so that it continues to grow. If you only harvest 30% of your kale when it comes time, this lets it quickly regrow. Doing this means that you can easily keep this superfood in your garden and in your diet.

HYDROPONICS

Lettuce

As you have been reading through this book, I would bet it's safe to say that no plant has popped up more often in our discussion than lettuce. This is because lettuce absolutely thrives in hydroponic growing conditions, which is great since lettuce can be used to make salads, give some texture and flavor to our sandwiches and burgers and is just an all-round versatile vegetable to have in the kitchen.

Growing lettuce offers a lot of variety. While lettuce prefers a cool temperature and a pH level between 6.0 and 7.0, it works in any of the hydroponic systems which you have made. For this reason, lettuce makes a great entry plant for getting into hydroponics. Lettuce only takes a couple of days to germinate but the time to harvest depends on what kind of lettuce you decided on growing. For example, loose-leaf lettuce only takes forty-five to fifty days to get to harvest. Romaine lettuce can take up to eighty-five days.

Peppers

Like tomatoes, peppers are technically a fruit but are so tightly linked to vegetable-based dishes and crops that many people think of them as vegetables. For that reason, we'll be looking at both peppers and tomatoes in this section. Peppers share a lot of similarities to tomatoes in their growing preferences. Peppers like a pH level between 5.5 and 6.0 and a temperature in the range of warm to hot.

You can start peppers from seed or seedling. It takes about two to three months for your peppers to mature. When considering what kind of peppers to grow, know that jalapeno, habanero, mazurka, fellini, nairobi and cubico peppers all do fantastic in hydroponic growing.

Radishes

Like lettuce, radishes are one of the easiest plants to grow, whether it be in a traditional soil garden or in a hydroponic setup. As suggested in the last chapter, radishes are best grown from a seed rather than seedling and it only takes between three to seven days to begin seeing seedlings from them. Radishes grow well in a setup with lettuce because both plants like cool temperatures and a pH level between 6.0 and 7.0.

What's really good about radishes is that they don't need any lights, unlike most plants. This means that if the cost of getting a light is too much for you right out the gate, radishes offer a way of trying out hydroponic gardening before dropping that cash. What's craziest of all is that radishes can grow super-fast, sometimes being ready to harvest within a month!

Spinach

Another plant that grows well in combination with lettuce and radishes is spinach. Spinach enjoys cool temperatures and a pH level between 6.0 and 7.0, so it fits in perfectly. It needs a little lighter than radishes do but it doesn't require very much at all.

It'll take about seven to ten days to go from seed to seedling with spinach and can be ready to harvest within six weeks. Harvesting can last up to twelve weeks depending on how you do. You can either harvest the spinach in full or you can pull off some leaves at a time.

This makes spinach another great option for those first getting into hydroponic gardening.

Tomatoes

Okay, okay, we all know that tomatoes are technically a fruit. But we're looking at it here because together with the rest of the vegetables in this section, add tomatoes and you have one great salad! Tomatoes will grow best in a hot environment and you will want to set up a trellis in your grow tray. They also like a pH level between 5.5 and 6.5.

HYDROPONICS

Tomatoes come in a variety; from the traditional ones we're looking at here through to those small cherry tomatoes that make delicious snacks. Germination can be expected between five to ten days and it will take a month or two before you begin to see fruit. You can expect it to take between fifty and a hundred days to be ready for harvesting and you will be able to tell by the size and color of the tomatoes.

Fruits

Nothing tastes sweeter than fruit that you have grown yourself. Hydroponic gardening offers a great way to grow some fruit inside the comfort of your own house. Like vegetables, there are many options available to us but we'll be focusing on those that grow the best.

<u>Blueberries</u>

Great for snacks, baking and even adding vitamins to your morning meal, blueberries are a fantastic crop to grow. However, blueberries can be quite difficult to germinate from seeds so it is recommended that you transplant blueberry plants instead. Blueberries are one of the slower plants to begin bearing fruit and can even take over a year to get to the point of producing. They

HYDROPONICS

like themselves a pH level between 4.5 and 6.0 in a warm climate.

Strawberries

The most popular of all the fruits that we can grow hydroponically, you can find strawberries being grown in smaller personal hydroponic setups and in the larger commercial growing operations. Preferring a warm temperature and a pH level of 6.0, strawberries grow best in a nutrient film technique system.

Strawberries that are grown from seeds can take up to three years to mature to harvesting levels, meaning that, like blueberries, they are a long-term crop.

HYDROPONICS

Together, blueberries and strawberries make for great fruit crops which can produce for several years if you are able to give them the growing time they need.

Herbs

Herbs make a great addition to any hydroponic setup. This is because it has been shown that herbs grown hydroponically have twenty to forty percent more aromatic oils than herbs that have been grown in a traditional soil garden. This means that you get more out of your hydroponic herbs with less used. This allows you to use less for the same end goal in your cooking, which means that your herbs will last you longer.

The best system for growing herbs is the ebb and flow system. Hydroponic herb gardens have been becoming a norm across the world because of their effectiveness. There are now even restaurants that grow their own hydroponic herb gardens on site because it is the most effective way to get fresh herbs of amazing quality.

Basil is the most popular of the herbs, with basil making up about 50% of the herb market in Europe. Both basil and mint like a warm environment and a pH level between 5.5 and 6.5. Similarly, chives prefer a warm to hot temperature and a pH sitting squarely around 6.0. This means that if you are careful with the temperature and pH level you can grow all three of these wonderful herbs in the same hydroponic setup.

An herb garden is a great way to get started with hydroponics. They can stay harvestable for incredibly long periods of time; they taste better than herbs grown in soil and make great additions to just about any meal. Not only that but herb gardens tend to be smaller than vegetable or fruit gardens and so a hydroponic herb garden will take up less space and can save some money in setup costs.

Hydroponic Nutrition

In this section, we'll turn our attention towards the nutrient solution which we use to fill up our reservoirs and provide our plants with what they need to continue to grow and stay strong. In order to get an understanding of this important component of our hydroponic systems, we will explore macro and micronutrients, the importance of researching the needs of our plants and how we go about mixing our own solution so that pH levels and electrical conductivity are in proper ratios.

What is a Nutrient Solution?

When we talk about the nutrient solution we use in our reservoirs, we are speaking about a properly proportioned liquid fertilizer. While there are a ton of commercial options available on the market today, we will be exploring how we go about mixing our own. This way, even if we decide to go with a store-bought option, we know how we can get the most control over our hydroponic garden's nutrition.

When it comes to growing plants, there are sixteen elements that combine together from the nutrients we use, our water and the oxygen in the air. A nutrient solution replaces those nutrients that would be found in the soil by combining them together into our water.

It is important to know what nutrients each of our plants want, as they are different from each other. There are more plants in this world than we can cover in one book, so it is important that you learn how to find this information for yourself. The best way to do this is to open up Google and search "name of plant + nutrient requirements hydroponic". If you were growing tomatoes then this would look like "tomato nutrient requirements hydroponic". Looking at the search results you will find that almost all of them are titled something like "Tomato fertilizer requirements" or "Tomato crop nutrition" and "What nutrients do tomato plants need?" Each of these sites will offer you the information you need. I recommend that you look at several sites rather than just one, to see if the needs change or if a particular site offers more specific information.

Primary Macronutrients

When we speak about primary macronutrients, we are referring to those nutrients that our plants require in large quantities. For humans, macronutrients are fat, protein and carbohydrates. While plants do care about these components, it is more for how they produce and handle them inside of themselves. When it comes to the nutrients they are after, our plants love nitrogen, phosphorus and potassium. We want to make sure that we have proper ratios of these big three so that our plants can stay at their healthiest, produce bigger yields and continue to grow.

Nitrogen

Found in amino acids, chlorophyll and nucleic acids, nitrogen is an element made up of enzymes and proteins. While humans like protein in its pure form, plants like it when they get it through nitrogen. If your plants aren't getting enough nitrogen then they will have a lower protein content. Too much nitrogen, on the other hand, leads to darker leaves and it adds to vegetative plant augmentation.

We want to make sure that our plants have a proper nitrogen balance because this will make sure that our plants are stronger, make better use of their own carbohydrates, stay healthier and manufacture more protein.

Phosphorus

Phosphorus is actually a major element in the RNA, DNA and ATP system of our plants. This is a lot of scientific jargon to say that phosphorus is super important to our plants. A deficiency of phosphorus can cause our plants to take longer to mature. Not only that but the poor plant growth and root growth can also lead to a reduced yield and see the plant's fruits drop off before they are mature. Likewise, too much phosphorus can lead to a lack of zinc (a micronutrient) in our plants.

Our plants want to be getting enough phosphorus so that they can better make use of photosynthesis. It also helps our plants in controlling cell division and in regulating how they make use of starches and sugars.

Potassium

The last of our three big macronutrients, potassium is slightly less important than nitrogen and phosphorus. This should not be taken as an excuse to ignore the potassium levels in our nutrient solutions. When our plants don't get enough potassium, they are at risk of having weaker stems and a reduced yield. Likewise, when we have too much potassium, we mess with the magnesium uptake of our plants.

When our plants are getting the right amount of potassium, we are making sure that they are using the water from our reservoirs to the best of their ability. Potassium also helps with our plants' resistance to disease, how they metabolize their nutrients and even how they regulate excess water.

Micronutrients

When we speak about micronutrients, we are referring primarily to seven different nutrients that our plants like to have. These are boron, chlorine, copper, iron, manganese, molybdenum and zinc. Together these micronutrients aren't nearly as important as our macronutrients but are still very important.

Typically, horticulturalists only add micronutrients when their plants show signs of some sort of deficiency. However, before you start adding micronutrients into your mixture, you want to make sure that the issue is actually with the nutrients themselves. For example, a deficiency can be caused by pests or poor pH levels. If we go adding micronutrients into our mixtures when the problem had nothing to do with the micronutrients, then we are risking damaging our plants. For this reason, you should first consider all the possible causes and rule out as many as you can before you start reaching for micronutrients.

Mixing Your Own Solution

The first thing we need to do when mixing our own solution is to figure out exactly what our plants need. We saw how we did this above in the section titled "What is a Nutrient Solution?" The information that you found in this section will let you know exactly what your plants want. We will take that information and use it here to fill out the specifics of this approach.

Before we get to mixing up our solution, we need to first go out and purchase some materials. We need to pick up some buckets. We need one bucket for each part of the solution. Three buckets tend to be a good number, as it allows us to tackle what they call an A, B, Bloom system. Some systems only require two buckets as there are only two steps to the mixture. You also want to buy a digital scale that can get down to hundredths of a gram. And of course, we need to purchase the nutrient salts that will be making up our solutions. These are salts which break down in water to give us the macronutrients we need. They can be bought at any hydroponic gardening store. Amazon.com also offers both premixed nutrient solutions and the raw nutrients you need to mix your own.

HYDROPONICS

You will also want to make sure that you have some clean measuring cups and some rubber gloves to keep yourself safe. You want to fill the buckets up with the proper amount of water needed for each part of the solution. This will depend on what kind of mix your particular plants need and so will be a personalized amount. When it comes to our water, we need to make sure that it is clean. It is always better to use a filtration system to get rid of contaminants that may be present in the water.

You weigh out the proper amount of nutrient salt using the scale. Once you have this amount you pour the salt slowly into the first bucket of water. Do it slowly to stop it from splashing and losing some of the solution in the process. You should see the salts begin to dissolve almost as soon as they touch the water. After you finish the first one, measure out the salts for your second part of the solution. Repeat until all parts of the solution have been mixed in their own buckets. You may want to put lids on them and give them a shake to make sure that there are no clumps of nutrients left undissolved.

After we have our mixture (or mixtures) ready, we need to check the pH level. We know that most plants prefer something between 5.5 and 6.5. Water is a neutral medium which means that it has a pH level of 7. Get yourself some pH level testers and be prepared to get to work. We need to bring the level down a little bit. This means we have to adjust the pH level by mixing in a solution that is designed to lower the pH. These solutions are highly acidic, so you should only use a little bit at a time. You want to dilute the pH lower solution, so mix a couple of drops of it into a gallon of water. This should give you a solution closer to 2.0 or so. The nutrients you use raise the pH level of the water so you need to start from 2.0 and increase as you add the mixture. You then slowly add this diluted mixture into your nutrient solution. Make sure that you add this slowly and stop to check the pH level often.

After your pH level is in line, you will need to check the electrical conductivity of the mixture. To do this you need to get yourself an electronic EC meter. Electrical conductivity lets us get an accurate reading of the balance of nutrients and pH level. Since we have mixed our own nutrient solution, we have had to use mineral salts to get the nutrients we desire. We can figure out the number of nutrients in the solution through electrical conductivity. Most plants want an EC of somewhere between 1.5 and 2.5 so this can be a great way to check and make sure we've got a proper mixture before we feed it off to our plants.

If we come in lower than 1.5, this means we don't have enough nutrients in our solution and so we will need to add more in order to bring it up. Likewise, if it is too high then we risk subjecting our plants to nutrient burn. Nutrient burn refers to the physical signs that our plants are getting too many nutrients. Leaf scorch is an obvious sign of nutrient burn. Root burn is also another common symptom of nutrient burn. We want to raise healthy plants, so this means we shouldn't be overfeeding them too many nutrients.

Once you've checked to see that the EC level is where you want it, you have successfully mixed your own nutrient solution. While the specifics depend on the plants you choose to grow, this outline should show you that it really isn't that hard to prepare our own solutions and keep close control over our hydroponic systems and the health of our plants.

HYDROPONICS

Chapter Summary

- We have a ton of options available to us when it comes to growing vegetables including beans, cucumbers, kale, lettuce, peppers, radishes, spinach and tomatoes.

- When it comes to fruits, blueberries and strawberries make great additions to a hydroponic garden.

- Herbs grow amazingly in hydroponic gardens, having up to forty percent more aromatic oils than soil-grown herbs. The most popular of these is basil but many herbs grow especially well in an ebb and flow system.

- A nutrient solution is a properly proportioned liquid fertilizer that we can either buy from the store or we can mix ourselves.

- When it comes to our plants, they want a lot of macronutrients. This macronutrient food group is made up of nitrogen, phosphorus and potassium.

- Micronutrients for plants are boron, chlorine, copper, iron, manganese, molybdenum and zinc. Before we start introducing micronutrients into our nutrient solutions, we should first take steps to make sure that the problem is actually related to a lack of micronutrients.

HYDROPONICS

- We want to make sure of this because we want to avoid subjecting our plants to nutrient burn, which is what happens when they have too many nutrients and it can really hurt their overall health.

- Always use filtered water and wear rubber gloves when you are mixing your own solution. For each step in your solution, use a separate bucket that you have sterilized.

- After you mix in your nutrient salts, check the pH level of the water. Most plants prefer a pH level between 5.5 and 6.5.

- The last step is to check the EC level of our solution. We want an EC level somewhere between 1.5 and 2.5.

In the next chapter, you will learn all about how to keep your hydroponic garden in great working order through regular check-ups and maintenance. This includes sanitizing and sterilizing your equipment and trays. You'll see how we keep our reservoirs clean and clear of any problems. We'll look at root disease and how to handle salt build-up before it kills off your plants. You'll learn how to tell when algae becoming a problem and when to clean it out and you'll learn all about problems with fruiting and flowering.

CHAPTER FIVE

MAINTENANCE OF YOUR HYDROPONIC GARDEN

By this point, we have made our hydroponic systems, picked out the plants we want to grow and mixed together a batch of nutrient solution to give them all the macronutrients they could ever desire. By now, it is safe to call yourself a hydroponic gardener! But the work hasn't finished yet. Now that you have your setup and you are growing your plants; you have to remain vigilant in maintaining your hydroponic garden.

This chapter is packed full of tools to help make sure that your garden continues to run smoothly. To this end, we'll look at how we sanitize our growing space, as well as how we go about sterilizing it. These two words are often used interchangeably but are actually two different steps. From there we will explore the ways we can keep our reservoirs in good condition, look at some general troubleshooting advice and speak on how our plants tell us that they need help. Because of how super important the information in this section is, we will close out the sections with a quick recap on the actions you should be taking for your garden.

Sanitizing

When it comes to sanitizing our hydroponic gardens, what we mean is that we are giving our garden a deep clean. It is as important to keep our gardens clean as changing a burnt-out lightbulb is or making sure that our nutrient solution is properly balanced. A proper sanitization will kill off and get rid of most microorganisms that can cause damage. Sanitizing doesn't mean that you are using a cleaning product or a chemical solution. While this can be a part of sanitizing, sanitizing can be as simple as a wipe down and the removal of any filth and dead plant matter.

The first step in sanitizing which you will want to take is to make sure that any spills, excess water or plant runoff is immediately cleaned up. You can purchase a wet/dry vacuum which can help in cleaning up spills but, while this is a useful tool, you can do this cleaning by hand as well. You want to make sure that you are getting these spills quickly and cleaning them up fully because the extra moisture on the floor can raise the room's humidity. A rise in humidity increases the risk that mold will take up residence in our systems. It also risks exposing our plants to rot, which is a plant's worst nightmare. Not only that, but spills can actually damage your floors which can lead to having to pay for repairs.

Any time you enter into the room in which you keep your hydroponic garden, you want to keep an eye out for any dead plant matter that you can find. You should take the time every day to check for fallen leaves and other dead plant matter. While it is easy to just check your grow tray and call it a day, make sure you check the floor around your garden as plant matter can easily escape and out of sight doesn't mean it isn't hurting your plants. These will fall into your grow tray or onto the floor around your garden. We want to clean up this dead plant matter because it is extremely enticing to mold and fungi. It is also extremely enticing to a variety of pests (we'll see how to deal with those in the next chapter). Make sure when you harvest your crops that you always get rid of old root and plant matter rather than leave it for later.

When it comes to facing problems with plant rot, a lot of gardeners never realize that the problem stems from the cleanliness of the grow room. In the last chapter, we saw that we want to make sure that the problem with our plants is not something else before we start adding micronutrients into our solutions. This is one of those situations where people jump to conclusions. However, one of the first things we should be checking is that we have kept a clean garden space.

If your hydroponic setup uses an intake filter, then you are going to want to inspect and clean that filter at least once a week or so. These filters help to keep dust, bugs and molds from getting into our growing trays. Routine cleaning of the intake filter will make sure that your system keeps maximum airflow. It will also be a way to get an early warning of any pests that are trying to get into your garden. Finding a pest on the intake filter gives you a head start on preventing them from messing up and damaging your garden.

Once every few months or so you should also take out the bulbs from your lights and give them a wipe. You should also do this with any glass you have such as when you use a reflector with your lights. Setting a schedule to do this, say, every three months, will allow you to plan it out ahead of time and to make sure that you don't neglect this cleaning. Harvesting can also be a great time to get at this cleaning, as when we harvest our plants, we tend to open up more space and make it easier to get at our equipment. Glass cleaners or isopropyl alcohol can be used to clean this glass. We want to keep up with this cleaning as grime can build up on our glass and lights and this can reduce the light output that we are able to give our plants.

You will also want to sanitize the hardware in your grow room about as often as you clean the glass. This means wiping down our pumps, hoses, all the stuff like that. You'll even want to wipe down the outside of your grow tray and your reservoir. If you have equipment that has exposed circuitry then you will want to get a couple of cans of compressed air so that you can clean these without damaging any of the electronics.

To recap: Clean up any spills as soon as they happen. Check for dead plant material once a day. Check your intake filters on a weekly basis. Every couple of months you should get in and clean the glass and bulbs used in your lighting setup. Around the time you clean your glass, you should also give any hardware you are using a quick clean, using compressed air on anything with exposed circuitry.

Sterilization

When it comes to cleaning, sterilization is a more involved process than sanitization is. We sterilize our equipment in order to kill off microorganisms like bacteria, spores and fungi. Because we are speaking on hydroponic systems with the assumption that they will be kept indoors, we will look at how we use chemical cleaners to sterilize our equipment. We can also use heat and filtration but these are more involved and complicated and are more useful for large-scale growing operations.

Unlike sanitization, we don't want to sterilize nearly as often. With sanitization, some of the practices are best

HYDROPONICS

used on a daily or a weekly basis. Sterilization should be used far less often because not only is it unnecessary but it can also hurt our system and our plants. For one, it takes more time and thought to sterilize and it can leave nasty by-products if we aren't careful to rinse properly afterward. When it comes to sterilization, we will be primarily looking at sterilizing our trays and reservoir, as well as the inside of any tubes we must clean.

The two most common chemical cleaners for sterilization are bleach and hydrogen peroxide. Bleach typically contains sodium hypochlorite as its active ingredient. This is the same chemical which is used to disinfect wastewater. While bleach makes for a great sterilizer, it can leave residual traces on our equipment and so if you choose to use bleach you should be prepared to double and triple rinse anything you cleaned using it. After you harvest your plants but before you set up the next batch to grow is a great time for a bleach bath. Using a mixture of one-part bleach to one part water, you should soak any air stones or other submersibles as well as your tray and reservoir. Make sure that you rinse these off two or three times, just to be extra sure that no harmful residue is left.

Hydrogen peroxide is actually just water that has an unstable oxygen molecule. This makes it a great chemical cleaner as instead of leaving behind a harmful residue it actually breaks down into water. Since water doesn't hurt our plants, using hydrogen peroxide means you don't have to worry as much about the double or triple rinsing that bleach requires. You can use a rag that has been soaked in 3% hydrogen peroxide to wipe down and clean your components. If you have a larger setup, you may consider creating a hydrogen peroxide solution that you can have run through the system. For this, you would want to keep it at about 35% hydrogen peroxide. If you run a hydrogen peroxide mix through your system, make sure that you send some water through to rinse afterward before you return your plants to the system.

To recap: You shouldn't sterilize too often as this can hurt your plants. A good time to sterilize is between harvesting and setting up the new crop. If you use bleach to sterilize, make sure you double or triple rinse afterward to prevent residue from hurting your plants.

Maintaining Your Reservoir

When it comes to our gardens, it is clear that we have a favorite section. All the greenery at the top is just so pretty and exciting to watch grow. It can be easy to maintain a habit of removing the dead leaves that have fallen because it is fun to poke around our plants and see how they are doing. But while it is easy to focus up top, we can't let ourselves forget about how important the bottom of our system is too. Without the reservoir of nutrient solution, our plants wouldn't get what they need to grow and we would just have one dead garden.

Our reservoirs are such an important part of our hydroponic systems that we should make it our mission to see that they are kept in the best possible shape. To do that, there are several steps and behaviors that we should adapt to make sure we stay on top of reservoir maintenance.

The first step we should take is making sure that our reservoirs are kept at a proper temperature. If we let our reservoirs get too hot then the levels of oxygen go down and create conditions for root rot to flourish. We want to keep our nutrient solution around 65-75 degrees. If our reservoirs are too cold, we can always get an aquarium heater or a heating pad to raise the temperature up. If our reservoirs are too hot then there are several options available to us. We can get a reservoir chiller, move our setups into the shade, or add some ice cubes to our solution. We also want to make sure that after we paint our reservoir black, we then add a coat of white paint to help reflect rather than absorb heat.

If your hydroponic garden is using a circulating system, then you are going to need to make sure that you check on your water levels and top up the reservoir. We lose water to evaporation and to processes that our plants undergo. This means that water loss is a part of the gardening experience and so we should be prepared to top up what is lost. This is especially important with smaller systems, as the loss of a little bit of water in a smaller system is a bigger deal.

Once every week or every other week you should consider changing out the water in your reservoir. This is a process that can get very specific for each garden. Knowing when it is time to change is something that you will grow into. But to start, assume every two weeks. Using your EC meter can help you to know when the time is right. While the EC reader will let us know how much fertilizer is in our solutions, it doesn't give us a breakdown of how much of each nutrient is left. Our plants don't use every nutrient the same way, some are absorbed and processed quicker than others. This means that even when we are checking levels with our EC meter and seeing that there are enough nutrients, we can actually have too much of one kind and not enough of another. When we change out our water, we are able to make sure that we provide our plants with a freshly balanced nutrient solution. It also gives us a chance to sanitize our reservoirs.

Speaking of our EC meters, we want to make sure we are doing regular EC checks. Of course, the numbers we are aiming for here depend on what plants we are growing. By this point, you should already have researched proper EC levels for your plant of choice. You also want to make sure to do regular pH level checks. We know that we want to keep our pH around roughly 5.5 to 6.5.

Finally, the most important step of all is to make sure you are checking your pumps regularly. You want to get on top of any build-ups that may be growing in your pumps. We want to do this because nothing kills off a garden faster than a broken pump. Making sure to clean out your pumps and clear away any nutrient build-ups will go a long way to keeping your garden healthy and keeping your reservoir working as intended.

To recap: Keep your reservoir between 65-75 degrees. Check the water levels and top them up often. Change the water out of your reservoir every other week. Use an EC meter and pH tests to keep your levels in check. Check your pumps regularly to prevent blockages.

Salt Build-up and Salt Burn

Have you ever seen a garden that has a white (or off-white) build-up of crystalline crust on the stems of the plants or the top of the growing medium? This is what is called a salt build-up and it is very bad for your plants. A salt build-up can lead to salt burn. Salt burn around the roots will lead to the stem at the base of the plant dying. This leads to wilting during the hotter moments of the day and it can even open this area of your plant up as the perfect feasting ground for disease.

Salt build-up happens when your growing medium loses moisture to evaporation at a faster rate than the plants are able to use up the nutrients. The moisture evaporates but the nutrients stay behind and jack up the EC levels in the medium. The good news is that salt build-up is easy to handle as long as you know that's what you're dealing with.

That white crust on the stems and top of your growing medium is a dead giveaway. If you are seeing that white crust and you notice that your plants have become stunted in their growth, have taken on a darker color or are growing uncharacteristically slow, then you should have all the signs you need to diagnose a salt build-up. One way you can confirm your suspicions is to take an EC reading of the solution that drains from your growing tray. If the EC reading increases on draining, you almost certainly have a salt build-up problem.

If you have identified a salt build-up as a problem in your garden, then you are going to want to flush your growing media. While some gardeners will flush their system with plain water, this can actually have a negative effect. If there is a crop already growing, the drop in osmotic pressure can cause the plants to take in a ton of moisture around the roots. This can lead to fruit splitting or the vegetative growth coming in soft and weak.

HYDROPONICS

A healthier approach to flushing the growing medium is to use a flushing solution that has been premixed, such as you can find at any hydroponic store. You can also flush with a nutrient solution that is at one third the regular strength. Depending on your setup, you may find yourself needing to do this flush every few weeks such as if you have an ebb and flow system in a warm climate where evaporation happens easily.

To recap: You can identify salt build-up by a white crust on the top of your grow medium and on the bottom of your plant stems. This happens because of evaporation that leaves the nutrients stuck there. Use a nutrient solution flush at one-third of regular strength in order to clear away the build-up.

Algae

If you are running a hydroponic garden, you will have to deal with algae at some point, I promise. Therefore, it is important that you know what to keep a lookout for. Algae will look like a slimy growth that clings onto the different parts of your setup. It can be brown, green, reddish or black. You shouldn't be surprised if you find long strings of algae in your system and you shouldn't be surprised if it seems like it just showed up out of nowhere. Algae can grow super-fast.

Algae also smells horrible. It has a moldy, earthy scent to it. When you get a ton of algae decomposing in your system, it will give off an unpleasant odor that can be a sign that you have a serious algae build-up on your hands.

Algae can be a real pain. First off, it is really quite disgusting looking. But far worse than its esthetical value and its smell is the fact that algae can easily block up your drippers, pumps and any other component of your hydroponic system that is prone to blockages. Like we saw, this can easily kill off your garden. Not only that but if you have a serious algae problem it can even block off your growing substrates and steal oxygen away from your plants. When this starts to happen, it can lead to an increase in the biological oxygen demand of your system. This means that your plants won't be getting enough oxygen and this can lead to their roots suffocating. If algae attach directly to your plants' roots, then it can leave your plants at risk for pathogens like Pythium.

HYDROPONICS

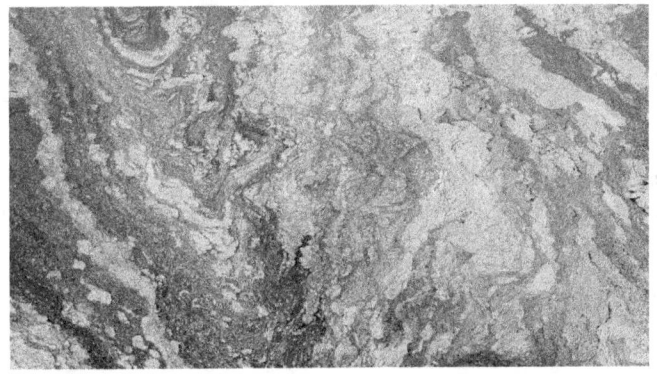

Algae itself can really suck but it gets even worse when it begins to break down and decompose. When this happens, it can actually release toxins into your system. These toxins then act as a food source for pathogenic fungi. When this begins to happen fungi can seem to just suddenly pop up and get a strong foothold in your system.

Most hydroponic growers tolerate a small number of algae in their systems because it can be difficult to get rid of. If you are taking care of your reservoir and making sure to clean it, then you can also take care of algae at this point. Make sure that you scrub down your systems between grows so that any algae that has gotten a foothold is removed. Some growers will use algaecide products in their nutrient solution to kill off algae but this can also cause our plants to be damaged. Not only that but algae regrow quite quickly after the use of algaecide products. This means that you will have to add in more algaecide soon afterward, thus risking your plants' health yet again.

To recap: A little bit of algae is fine but a major problem needs to be handled before it decomposes or it blocks up pumps and working components of your system. Clean by hand rather than using algaecides.

Maintaining Root Health

When it comes to the health of our roots, the most common killers are starvation, suffocation, damage from chemicals, pathogens, temperature or the EC/pH levels. The leading cause of root death and poor growing rates is suffocation. Many pathogens won't attack a healthy root system until they have been damaged due to poor conditions. Suffocation happens when there is a lack of oxygen getting to the plants such as when there is too much decomposing organic matter in our reservoirs, slow flow rates or too many plants all fighting to get enough oxygen.

As the roots begin to suffocate due to lack of oxygen, toxins will start to proliferate. Some plants will try to grow new roots to find alternative sources of oxygen but many will just up and die. If your plants aren't getting enough oxygen, consider adding an oxygen stone to your reservoir.

HYDROPONICS

If there aren't enough nutrients moving through your system, this will have an effect on the root system the same way that it affects the top part of the plant. However, it can be harder to tell that there is an issue with the roots. A lack of phosphate will cause the roots to turn brown and you will see a reduction in the number of lateral branches. A calcium deficiency causes the root system to thin out and develop a sickly brown color. Lack of manganese will lead to a root system that is shorter and finer than normal and you'll notice the tips of the roots browning. These each are clues that you want to take care of your nutrient solution and reservoir.

Another thing can lead to damaging our plants' roots are improperly balanced EC and pH levels. An unbalanced system will lead to severe stunting of the roots. At higher EC levels water will be lost from the roots and lead to root death. This is a common response from plants that enjoy a lower EC level. When pH levels get to be too high or too low then we can see root damage and problems with nutrient uptake. However, plants will take much kindlier to fluctuations in pH levels than they will in EC levels.

When it comes to root diseases, setups that use a recirculating system for the nutrient solution present the most risk. This is because the circulating of the solution can easily carry pathogens through to all of our plants. Some pathogens will attack the roots in a hydroponic system in a way that makes them easy to identify while others will seem almost invisible. Regardless if they show or not, all pathogens will lead to a reduction in the growth of your plants and the amount they yield. The most common pathogens that mess with our roots are didymella, verticillium, olpidium, plasmopara, pythium, fusarium and phytophthora.

Pathogens that affect your roots can come from a variety of sources. They can be airborne, waterborne, found in your growing medium, arrive from insects and pests, infected plant matter or even from seeds and dust. While airborne pathogens that damage your roots are rare, they can still happen. One of the most common sources for infection comes from soil. Soil can get into a hydroponic system from your hands, shoes, dust in the air, from our equipment or even from the water we use in our reservoir.

Root diseases and the pathogens that cause them like to attack plants that are already undergoing a lot of stress. Because stressed plants leave your system open to attack, the best way to defend against these pathogens is to make sure that your crop is healthy and not undergoing undue stress such as when we trim stems too often. Another cause of stress is our roots not getting enough oxygen, such as when algae has grown into a major problem.

One of the best behaviors we can get into is making sure that we take the time to check on the root system of our plants. Most of us want to poke around on the top part where it's all green and pretty. While it is important that we take care of our tops, we must not forget the bottom. Checking the roots on a regular basis will be a great tool for catching a problem before it becomes a crisis. If your plant is wilting or looks discolored then you should make sure to check the root system.

If you identify that a plant has or potentially has root disease, then your first step should be to remove it from the garden and destroy it. If a plant is diseased and you leave it in the system, you risk that disease being carried to the other healthy plants. These pathogens can survive and go from one crop to the next, so it is important that you sanitize and sterilize your hydroponic system between crops.

To recap: Root health is just as important as the health of our tops. A lack of oxygen is the most common problem for our roots. Avoid stressing the plants by doing regular checks of the EC and pH levels. Identify issues with roots so that you can remove diseased plants before they spread to healthy plants.

Fruiting and Flowering

When it comes to problems with our crops fruiting and flowering there can be a lot of different causes. These range from a lack of fruit development through to physiological disorders such as blossom end rot. You may find your fruits have skin disorders like blotches, streaks, silvering or uneven color. Another issue is fruit splitting which leads to ugly looking plants that are horribly misshapen.

Many hydroponic crops will begin to flower and fruit when they reach a proper age. If there is a problem with the fruiting, you may run into a problem with flower dropping. This is when the flowers and fruits drop off the plant before they are ready. This can be caused by external problems but it can also be internal such as when our plants are undergoing an undue amount of stress. A lot of crops will run into flower drop if the air temperatures are too high. The point at which heat affects plants is different for each kind. If your plants aren't getting enough light, this can also lead to flower drop. A lack of light also can stunt the growth of the whole plant.

Flower drop can also be caused by nutrient deficiencies. Common causes of flower drop due to deficiency are when our plants aren't getting enough nitrogen or phosphorus from the nutrient solution we have made. Stress caused by water can also lead to flower drop. This is stress caused by a poor irrigation system or from having an EC level that is too high. For this reason, we want to make sure that we are checking the EC levels of our nutrient solutions on a regular basis.

Another cause of fruit drop is when the weight of the fruit is too heavy for the plant to hold onto. This can be due to the weight of the fruit or the weight of the vegetative growth itself. For this reason, we want to make sure that we are trimming our plants in a healthy manner that promotes a manageable growth such as when we top our plants. When there are larger fruits growing on our plants, this can lead to the dropping of smaller fruits. This can actually serve to help the healthier, larger fruits to continue growing. Likewise, we may consider removing smaller fruits so that the energy spent growing them is redirected.

To recap: Issues with flowering and fruiting tend to be related to stress. Make sure to take good care of your plants, remove unhealthy fruits and give heavy plants support to prevent dropping.

HYDROPONICS

Chapter Summary

- Sanitizing refers to giving our systems a deep clean.

- Clean any spills as soon as they happen to prevent the moisture from messing with the room's humidity.

- Check for dead plant matter daily. This matter becomes a breeding ground for molds, fungi and bacteria.

- Clean your intake filter once a week or so to keep them in working order and get early warnings about possible pests.

- Every few months clean the bulbs and glass used in your lighting setup.

- Clean down your pumps, hoses and other hardware when you clean your bulbs.

- Sterilization is a more involved process but shouldn't be overused as it can damage your plants.

- Bleach and hydrogen peroxide can both be used to sterilize. If you use bleach make sure you double and triple rinse to remove all harmful residue.

HYDROPONICS

- Make sure that you keep your reservoir at a temperature of between 65-75 degrees.

- Top off the water levels in your reservoir as they get lower.

- Change the water in your reservoir every other week to keep tight control over the amount of nutrients in your solutions.

- Do regular EC and pH level checks.

- Check your pumps often to avoid blockages and breakdowns.

- Salt build-up can be identified by a layer of white crust on the top of your growing medium and the stems of your plants.

- Salt build-up happens when water evaporates from our solution and leaves its nutrients to build up.

- Salt build-up can lead to salt burn which can kill off parts of our plants and leave them at risk of pathogens.

- To deal with a salt build-up, flush your system with a nutrient solution at one-third of its regular strength.

HYDROPONICS

- Algae is a disgusting smelling, slimy growth (that can be green, red, black or brown) that grows in your reservoir.

- A serious algae problem can block up pumps and drippers and rotting algae can release toxins into your system.

- A small number of algae is typical in a hydroponic system, just make sure you scrub down and remove any algae every so often.

- You can use algaecide products to kill off the algae but this can also hurt your plants so if it isn't a huge build-up it can be best to wait until the next time you clean your reservoir.

- The most common cause of root damage is suffocation from a lack of oxygen.

- A lack of properly balanced nutrients will hurt your plants' roots just as much as it will hurt the tops.

- Improper EC and pH levels can also lead to root death, so make sure to keep an eye on your levels.

- Recirculating systems are at a bigger risk of spreading root-based diseases among your plants.

- Be careful about how much dirt is in your hands and clothing when you look after your garden as

HYDROPONICS

this is the key way for pathogens to get into your system.

- Root disease prefers to attack plants already under a lot of stress, so the best way to prevent root disease is to take proper care of your plants.

- Make sure you check your roots often and remove and destroy any plant showing signs of root disease.

- Pathogens can survive from one crop to the next, so always sterilize between crops.

- If there is a problem with fruiting, you may see flower dropping or fruit splitting.

- The most common cause of these fruiting problems is stressed out plants.

- Nutrient deficiencies can also be responsible for flower drop.

- Flower and fruit drop can also be caused by the weight of the fruit, so a trellis can help prevent this.

In the next chapter, you will learn all about the different kinds of pests that can try to take up a foothold in your garden. Along with a look at the pests themselves, you will learn how we take care of them so that we can keep our hydroponic gardens in the best shape possible.

CHAPTER SIX
PEST CONTROL

We've made it through setting up our own hydroponic garden, picking plants, learning about nutrients and figuring out how we can maintain it. But now we've come across a whole new issue: Pests. Our setup provided a great environment for our plants to grow. But it also created an environment which pests love and we even filled it with tons of healthy plants for them to eat. This would be fine if they provided some kind of service to our plants but all they want to do is snack on them and leave them wilted and yellowed.

In this chapter, we'll take a look at the most common pests that hydroponic growers encounter and we'll see how you can spot them in your own garden. Our number one defense against pests is to prevent them from making our gardens their home in the first place, so we will learn some of the techniques used to detect them early and prevent an infestation.

HYDROPONICS

Pests aren't the only problem we face as hydroponic growers. Disease is also something we must be vigilant in spotting, identifying and handling. To this end, we'll look at some of the more common diseases and how we can prevent them. A lot of this information was covered in chapter five, so we will be referring to it often here.

Common Hydroponic Pests

While there are many pests that can try to make our gardens their home, there are certain pests that show up with more regularity than others. These pests fall into five key categories: spider mites, thrips, fungus gnats, whiteflies and aphids. If you find yourself with an infestation of pests, it is a safe bet that they'll fall into one of these five categories.

Spider Mites

Out of all five types of pest, spider mites are a particularly annoying one. While they are less than a millimeter long, these little guys are actually tiny spiders. Because they are so small, they have a tendency to start damaging your plants before you even notice that they have taken up in your garden. Spider mite damage will look like tiny brown and yellow spots on the leaves of your plants. While they don't look like anything serious when there are only a couple of bites, this damage adds up quickly to really wreak havoc on your garden.

To spot a spider mite infestation, there are two key signs to look out for. While the damage on your plants can be a telltale sign, it doesn't specifically tell you that spider mites are the problem. To spot a spider mite infestation you should check your plants to see if you can spot any spider-like webbing. Another way to check for spider mites is to use a tissue or clean rag to gently wipe the bottoms of your leaves. If you come away with streaks of blood, this will tell you that you have a spider mite problem.

One way of handling spider mites is to wash your plants down with a hose or powerful spray bottle. The force of the water can often knock the mites off of your plant and drown them in the growing medium. Spider mites also have some natural enemies ranging from ladybugs to lacewings and you may consider adding these beneficial insects to your garden to feed on the spider mite population.

Aphids

These little guys are also known as plant lice. And just like head lice, they aren't all that much fun. These tiny, soft-bodied pests are pretty much able to set up in any environment. They multiply quicker than rabbits, so you want to make sure to tackle an aphid infestation as soon as possible. These pests are typically a quarter of an inch in size and can come in green, yellow, pink, black or gray varieties.

HYDROPONICS

Aphids like to feed on the juices of the plant and you can find them chewing on stems, leaves, buds, fruits or roots. They are particularly drawn to the newest parts of the plant. If you find that your leaves are misshapen or yellowing, checking the bottom can reveal aphids. They also leave behind a sticky substance referred to as honeydew. This sweet substance can actually attract other kinds of pests so aphids are particularly annoying little critters. This substance can also lead to the growth of fungus, like sooty mold which can cause your branches or leaves to turn an unpleasant black color. Aphids are also able to carry viruses from one plant to another so they can help nasty pathogens to spread quicker.

Like spider mites, spraying water on the leaves can dislodge them and leave them with a hard time finding their way back to your plants. If the infestation is large, dusting your plants with flour can constipate them and help convince them it is time to move on. Wiping down your plants with a mixture of soapy water can also help to kill and drive them off.

Thrips

Like spider mites and aphids, these little guys are also tiny. Often, they are only around 5 millimeters long. It can be hard to spot these little guys but they leave damage that is clear as day. If you start to see little metallic black specks on your leaves, you probably have some thrips snacking off your garden. Leaves that thrips attack will often turn brown and become super dry because the thrips like to suck out their juices.

HYDROPONICS

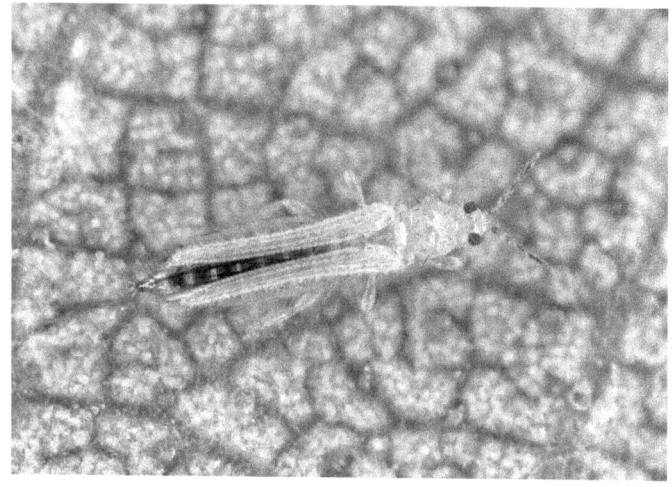

Thrips are small and are either black or the color of straw. They have slender bodies and two pairs of wings. Because they are so small, they look like dark threads to the naked eye. They like to feed in large groups and will fly away if you disturb them. They stick their eggs into flowers and leaves and they only take a couple of days to hatch so a thrip infestation can feel like it just happened out of the blue.

Because thrips like to lay their eggs in plants, it is super important that you remove any dead or fallen plant matter. If you paid attention in the last chapter, you'll know you should be doing this anyway as it helps to prevent many issues that can assail our hydroponic gardens. Make sure that you inspect your plants for thrip damage and remove any that are infested. Hosing off the plants will also help to reduce their population. Ladybugs, lacewings and minute pirate bugs all feed on thrips and can be beneficial to your garden.

Fungus Gnats

Fungus gnats are an odd one. Adult fungus gnats have no interest in harming your garden. But their larvae enjoy chewing on the roots of your plants which slows growth and opens the plant up for infection. In extreme cases, fungus gnat larvae can actually cause the death of plants. They really like areas with a lot of moisture and a high humidity. You'll likely notice adult fungus gnats before you have any issue. As adults, these gnats are about three millimeters in length and kind of look like mosquitos. They tend to be a grayish-black color with a pair of long legs and clear wings. Their larvae have shiny black heads with a whitish-transparent body.

HYDROPONICS

Adults typically live for a week and in that time lay up to 300 eggs. It takes half a week for the larvae to emerge but when they do, they start a two-week diet where their main dish is the roots of your plants. When they feed on your plants, they cause them to wilt, stunt their growth and cause a yellowing of their leaves. These nasty little things can have many generations living off the same plant.

If you suspect a fungus gnat infestation than you should inspect your plants by carefully turning up the soil around their stems and look for larvae. If you check a plant and it suddenly let's loose a bunch of adult gnats then you should dispose of that plant. They really like damp soils so make sure you aren't overwatering your plants. If you have a fungus gnat problem then letting your potting medium drain longer will help to kill off the larvae and mess up the development of fungus gnat eggs.

You can also spray your plants with a combination of peppermint, cinnamon and sesame oils. This mixture is called flying insect killer and will help to get rid of gnats.

Whiteflies

About the same size as spider mites, whiteflies look like small white moths that take up residence on your plants. They are easier to spot but because they fly away when you bother them they can be hard to kill. Like aphids, they enjoy sucking the juices out of your plant and you see their damage as white spots and yellowing of the leaves.

They tend to lay 200-400 eggs in clusters on the underside of the higher leaves. These eggs hatch in about a week and unattractive little nymphs come out that crawl around on your leaves before they grow wings. These crawlers will spread out from the egg and find a place to start chewing on your leaves. They'll stay in that spot for the next week or so before growing into young adults which will repeat the cycle of movement-feasting.

HYDROPONICS

Ladybugs and lacewings enjoy eating whiteflies and so introducing them to your garden can help to kill off whitefly populations. Hosing off plants with a strong blast of water will help in reducing their numbers as well. There are a bunch of organic pesticides on the market which you can get to deal with whiteflies. These pesticides can also work for the other pests but pesticides should be a last resort option, one that you are careful with so as not to lead to undue stress on your plants.

Preventing Pests

Now that we have an idea of the pests that are most common to hydroponic gardens, let us turn our attention towards how we prevent these pests from getting into our gardens in the first place. Many of these techniques will help us to identify a possible infestation as it is trying to get started and so they offer us early warnings to prepare ourselves to battle pests. If we keep up our preventative measures and keep our eyes peeled for pests then we can save our plants a lot of damage and ourselves a lot of time by cutting off the problem at the head.

When it comes to pests it is also important to understand that not every pest is the same. This doesn't just mean that whiteflies are different from fungus gnats. What this means is that fungus gnats on the West coast are going to be different than fungus gnats on the East coast. Not every solution for prevention or extermination will work. A certain pesticide may be used to kill gnats on the East but the ones on the West might have grown an immunity to it. For this reason, it is important to check with your local hydroponics store to see if there is any region-specific information you need to tackle your pest problem.

One of the ways that we prevent pests is to make sure that we limit their ability to enter our garden in the first place. We can do this a few ways. Insect screens go a long way to keeping out pests. We also want to limit the amount of traffic in and around our setups. If at all possible, our setups will benefit greatly if they can be protected by airlock entrances as these offer the most secure protection against both pests and pathogens. Airlocks can be doubled up to create a space before the garden in which to wipe down dirt and any insects or eggs that are catching a free ride on your clothing.

In order to see if pests are starting to show up in your garden, use sticky traps around your plants. Yellow and blue sticky traps are both useful, as they attract different pests, so you want to make sure to use both kinds for the best results. Place traps near any entrances into your garden such as doors or ventilation systems. Also, make sure to place one or two near the stems of your plants to catch those pests that prefer snacking on the lower bits, such as aphids or fungus gnats. Get into the habit of checking these traps regularly as they can give you a great idea of what kind of life is calling your garden home.

While traps will help us to get a head start fighting any infections, they aren't a foolproof method when it comes to avoiding pests. Traps should be used together with personal spot checks. This means that you should be checking your plants for pests a couple of times a week. Take a clean cloth and check the bottom of your leaves. Check around the roots for any fungus gnat larvae. You can check the tops of leaves visually. Look for any signs of yellowing or bite marks as described above.

Make sure to remove any weeds that take up root in your garden as these plants are only going to sap your garden's resources and offer a breeding ground for pests. Also remove dead or fallen plant matter, of course. This includes leaves but also any fruit, buds or petals that have been dropped.

Finally, before you introduce any new plants to your garden, make sure to quarantine them first so that you can check them for pests. You can use a magnifying glass to get a closer look if you need to. Give the new plants a thorough inspection, making sure to check all parts of the plant and the potting soil before you transfer it over.

By creating a system and a schedule for inspecting your plants, you can prevent an infestation of pests from ruining your garden or causing you a lot of headaches. A vigilant eye will give you the upper hand in both preventing and dealing with any kind of problem you have with pests. Remember, a strong defense is the best offense when it comes to keeping your plants healthy and free from harm.

Common Hydroponic Diseases

Disease is awful whether we're speaking about humans or about our plants. In the last chapter, we saw how we maintain a healthy garden so as to prevent pathogens from taking hold in our systems. Here we will look at the most common diseases that hydroponic growers find themselves facing.

Iron Deficiency

When your plants don't get enough iron they won't be able to produce enough chlorophyll. This means that their leaves will turn bright yellow with bold green veins. If left untreated, the leaves will start to turn white and then begin to die. This will result in a stunting of growth and a dying back of the plant as a whole. These signs of iron deficiency look a lot like some of the other diseases so it is important that you confirm it is an iron deficiency before you begin treatment.

HYDROPONICS

To diagnose an iron deficiency, you are going to want to test your growing operation. Do a pH test and check the numbers. Higher than 7.0 can cause many plants to stop absorbing iron. Also, do an EC reading and check your levels; you may have an imbalance. Remember that an EC check doesn't confirm how many of each nutrient is in your solution so you may consider changing out the nutrient solution for a freshly balanced batch.

If you have identified an iron deficiency, the first thing you should do is fix the pH and EC levels and get that all within the proper range. You can also buy liquid iron which you use to spray down your plants. Spray the liquid iron directly on the leaves. Liquid iron is only a quick fix and not the solution, so if it shows results then consider tweaking your nutrient solution to include more iron.

Powdery Mildew

Powdery mildew is an easily recognizable fungal disease. Caused by fungal species, this disease thrives on plants in areas with less moisture in the growing medium and it especially loves it when the humidity levels are high on the surface of your plants. This mildew begins on the younger leaves of plants and it looks like little blisters all over them. These blisters are slightly raised and they lead to your leaves curling up. This curling exposes the lower parts of the leaf's structure for easier access. Leaves that have been infected look like they are coated in an unsightly white powder. Left untreated the leaves will turn brown and fall off. It primarily attacks new leaves and so the older, more mature leaves of your plant will tend to be free of infection.

To deal with powdery mildew, you want to prune away some of the plant to open it up to better airflow. This will help to reduce the humidity of the plant so as to make it less inviting to powdery mildew. Remove any foliage that is already infected and make sure to clean up any fallen plant matter. A spray made of 60% water and

HYDROPONICS

40% milk can be used once every two weeks to help prevent powdery mildew from taking hold. Also wash your plants from time to time, as this will help prevent both powdery mildew and a variety of pests. A fungicide can be applied if the problem is extreme but this also risks hurting the plants.

Gray Mold

Gray mold goes by a variety of names such as ash mold or ghost spot. Regardless of the name you call it, you can spot it easily. It begins as little gray spots on your plants that start to turn into a fuzzy gray abrasion that eats away at your plant until it's entirely brown and nothing more than a disgusting mush. Gray mold can be found on a bunch of plants but it is particularly familiar to anyone that has grown strawberries as it completely ruins the berries it infects.

HYDROPONICS

Gray mold likes to settle in near the bottom of the plant and in the areas that the plant shadows the most. It tends to begin on flowers that have wilted and then it quickly spreads out to the leaves and stem. It really likes those areas with a high humidity. The infected plants will begin to rot away and if left untreated, gray mold is one of the most disgusting diseases to have to deal with. The spores like cool temperatures and high humidity and they can get into the healthy tissue of the plants directly so your plants are especially susceptible after a trimming.

Pruning your plants or setting up on with a trellis helps to improve the air circulation and lower the humidity of your plants so that gray mold will desire them less. You can also use a small fan to increase the airflow around your plants. Always remove any fallen plant matter. If you spray your plants down in the morning, give them time to dry so that gray mold is less interested in the bed. Fungicides can also help in tackling gray mold infections.

Preventing Disease

We saw in the last chapter how we maintain our hydroponic gardens. These steps are also important because they help us to prevent disease from taking hold in our gardens. Because they are directly related to our conversation here in this chapter, you will recognize a lot of this information. However, it is of vital importance in keeping disease out of your garden so it is worth restating.

The most important thing we can do to help our plants avoid becoming diseased is to make sure that they are healthy and not overly stressed. This means we want to check our pH and EC levels regularly to make sure that they are in the proper range. We also want to make sure that we clean our reservoir from time to time and have a schedule for cycling out the old solution and filling it back up with a new, freshly balanced one. This will help your plants to stay healthy which helps them to fend off attacks by pathogens.

You also want to keep your garden as clean as possible. Like with pests, using a two-door airlock system will give you an area in which to wipe down and clean up before you enter into the garden. Doing this helps to remove dirt from your person, which is absolutely the leading way for pathogens to get introduced into your setup. Make sure to clean your hands and any tools you plan to use in the garden before you start messing around. Also, clean off your boots and consider removing any jacket or outdoor wear that you have on.

Clean up any spills as soon as they happen to avoid introducing extra moisture and humidity around your plants as these attract disease. Also make sure that you are removing any dead plant matter as soon as you spot it. Dead plant matter becomes a breeding ground for both pests and disease. Check your plants for disease regularly and remove any that show signs of heavy infection. Consider washing your plants down twice a week or so to knock off any pests or infection that may be trying to take hold.

By keeping vigilant and maintaining your garden, you can prevent disease from taking hold and ensure that you are raising healthy, beautiful crops.

HYDROPONICS

Chapter Summary

- Pests can be one of the most annoying parts of tending a hydroponic garden but proper care will help to prevent infestation.

- Spider mites are tiny spiders that eat away at your plants and cause tiny brown and yellow spots all over the leaves.

- Spider mites can be identified by the spider-like webbing they leave behind or trails of blood left behind when you wipe the bottoms of leaves.

- You can deal with spider mites by hosing off your plants or introducing beneficial insects into your garden.

- Aphids are little lice-like pests that feed off the juices of your plants and leave them misshapen, yellowed and covered in a sticky substance known as honeydew.

- Spraying down the plants can help to dislodge aphids. A dusting of flour on your plants will constipate any aphids and help to start them migrating away from your garden. A soapy water mixture can also be used to kill them off.

- Thrips are tiny creatures that leave little metallic black specks all over the leaves of your plants.

HYDROPONICS

- Thrips lay their eggs inside your plants, so hose off your plants, remove any infested plants and consider introducing beneficial insects to the garden to eat the thrips.

- Fungus gnats don't harm your garden when they are in their adult stage but their larvae snack on the roots of your plants which causes them to wilt, yellow and causes stunting of growth.

- Fungus gnat larvae take up in your growing medium, so check the plant beds for infestation. If a plant sends up a bunch of adult gnats, you can assume it to be infected and dispose of it. Spraying your plants with flying insect killer can help take care of gnats as well.

- Whiteflies look like little moths and they love sucking your plants dry, leaving them with white spots or yellowing of the leaves.

- Introduce beneficial insects to the garden to deal with whiteflies. Hosing off plants also helps and organic pesticides serve as a last-ditch effort against them.

- Always check with your local hydroponic or gardening store to see if pests in your area are immune to any of the known treatment options.

HYDROPONICS

- Limiting access to your garden will help to limit the chances of infestation. Screen doors and airlocks offer great protection.

- Set up blue and yellow traps in and around your garden, making sure to have some around the stem of your plants. These give early warnings of infestation.

- Check your plants and spray them off with water from time to time. A thorough check twice a week should be enough.

- If you are planning to introduce a new plant into your garden, make sure that you quarantine it and check it thoroughly for infestation and infection before you plant it.

- Iron deficiency causes your plants to have dark green veins and yellowing of the middle. Check pH and EC levels for signs of problems. Spray liquid iron to see if it helps and consider introducing more iron into your nutrient mix.

- Powdery mildew is like a white dusting on top of your plants that can cause leaves to die off. Open the plant to better airflow, remove any infected foliage and consider a milk-water spray as well as washing the plants from time to time.

- Gray mold is the grossest of the diseases and the easiest to spot. Prune plants to open them up to better airflow, remove dead plant matter or infected matter and consider using a fungicide.

- Preventing disease is best done by keeping our plants nice and healthy. If you follow the steps outlined in chapter 5, check your plants for signs of infection and take care of them with scheduled washes then you should be able to prevent major harm from coming to your garden.

In the next chapter, we will look at some of the mistakes that new growers are prone to make and see how we can avoid making them ourselves. We'll also look at some of the myths surrounding hydroponic growing to dispel any false ideas we may still have about it.

CHAPTER SEVEN

MYTHS AND MISTAKES TO AVOID

Our time together has almost come to a close. Before you go out and get going on your own garden, let us take the time to look at some of the mistakes and myths that pop up frequently in discussions on hydroponic gardening. By digging through the myths to find the truth and learning from the mistakes of those that came before us, we are able to benefit from the knowledge and avoid making the same mistakes ourselves.

Mistake: Hard-to-Use Setups

When you are setting up your hydroponic garden, it is important that you consider how hard it will be to use. Are you going to have a difficult time reaching the plants in the back because you put the garden up against a wall? Are you going to bump into the lights every time you try to tend the bed because the space is too small and cramped?

When you are setting up your garden it is important that you consider issues such as the physical space in which it will sit. You want to make sure that you can get to all your plants without a struggle. If you're knocking over lights or throwing your back out to reach plants then the setup isn't going to be a very good one. Chances are you are going to end up breaking something or neglecting it. Consider the ways in which you move through the garden space; make sure that you are able to reach everything.

You also want to make sure that you are able to get to your reservoir easily. While it may be tempting just to rest the grow tray on top of the reservoir, consider how this might cause issues when it comes time to switch the nutrient solution. Will you have somewhere to place the grow tray while you have to mess around with the reservoir? If not, then how did you plan to do it?

We saw in chapter five all the different steps we take to maintain our hydroponic garden. Read those steps again before you set up your garden and make sure that your setup allows you to actually get in the garden and take those actions. If not, then you will want to reconsider your design.

Myth: Hydroponic Gardens Are Only for Illegal Substances

It seems that any time hydroponics pop up in the news it is in relation to some illegal grow operation that has been busted by the police. This has led to a stigma around hydroponics, one which it really doesn't deserve. Just because it happens that a lot of illegal growers use hydroponic setups, it doesn't mean that hydroponics is used just for illegal purposes.

As we saw above, we went an entire book looking at hydroponics and never once did we mention any drugs. We looked at how hydroponics will help our herb gardens to produce 30% more aromatic oils. We talked about vegetables and fruits. Never once did we speak about illegal substances.

This is because hydroponics is a system for growing plants. Those plants don't need to be illegal. They can be, yes. But they can also be the garden veggies you serve in a salad. Hydroponics is just a great system for growing plants and it is a system that you can run from inside your house, which means that you can hide your garden easily. But hydroponics itself is not illegal, it does not mean that you are taking part in illegal activities and this particular myth should be put to rest already.

HYDROPONICS

Mistake: Choosing the Wrong Crops for Your Climate

You hear about a new crop on one of the gardening sites you check online. It sounds like it could be a lot of fun to grow, some kind of berry you never heard of before and people say it does great in a hydroponic setup. You order some seeds, plant it and it grows but it just doesn't give the results you wanted. Looking to see what goes wrong, you do some more Googling on the plant and you realize it needs to be in a super-hot, arid environment. And you're living through the coldest winter of your life.

Different plants want different climates and nothing will be more disappointing than trying to grow a plant that just doesn't like the climate you can offer. We should always do our research on the plants that we want to grow. We can do this easily with Google or by going into our local hydroponic store to speak to the staff.

Myth: Hydroponics Have to be Done Indoors

We've spoken a lot about indoor hydroponics in this book. This was a choice to highlight the fact that we can raise hydroponics indoors. There any many people out there who don't have access to an outside plot in which to start a garden. Most people that live in an apartment building have at best a balcony and many don't even have that much. Being that you can have an indoor garden, hydroponics offers a way for more people to get into gardening.

But this doesn't mean that you can't have an outdoor hydroponic garden. When we raise our gardens indoors, we are able to control the seasons and really take an active role in maintaining the humidity and temperature, how long the grow lights are on and much more. If we grow outdoors then we can save money on grow lights by using the sun but we also open our garden up to more risk from pests and disease. However, hydroponics can be done anywhere that you want.

Mistake: Picking the Wrong Plants for Your Setup

This could also be called "Not Doing Your Research." Like picking plants that match your climate, you are also going to want to make sure you pick plants that will work well in your setup. Some plants work better in different systems. Some want less water; some want slower draining and others want more water and others yet want faster draining.

It is important that you research the plants that you want to put in your garden. There are hundreds upon hundreds of websites jam-packed with information about every plant you could consider growing. They will tell you the pH and EC levels for the plant, how hot they like their environment, how much water they want and what type of hydroponic setup is best for them. We looked at a handful throughout this book but there is no way we could have covered all of them. But Google is your friend.

So make sure you do your research and plan out your garden. Preparing yourself with information will avoid costly mistakes. Not only does it cost to grow but there is also a time cost and you will lose weeks before you realize that growing that one plant is a losing battle.

Myth: Hydroponics is Super Expensive

This myth has good reason to be around. The truth is that hydroponics can be expensive. Can be. But just because it can be doesn't mean that it always is. When you head to the hydroponic store and look at all the prices and get talked into buying more than you really needed, then it is going to be expensive. But like many hobbies, it depends on how serious you want to take it and you can always start slow.

There are a ton of ways to cut down costs when beginning your garden. Searching online you can find hundreds of do-it-yourself guides to starting a hydroponic setup. We looked at three pretty cheap options ourselves in chapter two. These offer great ways to try out hydroponic gardening for the new grower. You can get your hands dirty and really see if it is something that you enjoy before you go spending a lot of money. Speaking of spending a lot of money…

Mistake: Scaling Up the Operation Too Early

Starting off too big can be a terrible mistake. For one, it means sinking a lot of money into growing right out the gate. Before you do this you should at least have some experience with hydroponics. Another big issue is that until you have some experience you don't actually know how to best care for your garden and every step in the operation cycle is going to be a learning experience. This isn't bad when we start small but starting bigger means any mistakes we make along the way are going to cost us that much more.

You should start slow and learn the ropes. As you go along you can buy more expensive equipment as you figure out what equipment you actually need and what equipment works best with your style of growing. As you learn the way your plants take to the system, get a feel for how they grow in your setup, then you can begin to expand. You can start to add in another grow tray, maybe two. But add slowly, take your time and make sure you have a good grasp of how to run a small garden before you jump into a large one. You can always get there but patience will help save you from some truly devastating mistakes along the way. It's one thing to mess up one grow tray, it's another to mess up a dozen.

Myth: Hydroponics is Unnatural

What happened to just sticking a plant in the ground and letting it grow? Hydroponics seems like a lot of work to do the same thing. The plants come out bigger, too. Seems like there must be something unnatural going on here. It must be all those chemicals used in the solution.

Of course, this myth is just silly. We are growing plants and using natural mix in our grow trays. We mix together a nutrient solution but all of these are natural nutrients that the plants take from the Earth anyway. Hydroponics is just a system of growing. We grow healthy plants the same as any gardener tries to. There are no gross chemicals being used to give us better growth than soil. All we are doing is using the natural desires of the plant to provide it with the most comfortable growing experience we can.

In a way, hydroponics is almost like owning a pet. There are wild dogs in the world but nobody thinks it is unhealthy to have a pet dog. We are treating our plants the same; we are providing for their needs so that they can focus on living. Just in the case of plants, living means growing into fruit or vegetables that we can enjoy afterward!

Mistake: Not Maintaining Your Garden

I know, I know. You've heard this one before. But it is the number one mistake that new growers make and so we are going to speak about it one last time. The fact is that maintaining your garden doesn't just mean changing the water. It doesn't just mean we look at the garden when the plants look ill and infected and get to work. Maintaining our gardens is a commitment that any gardener has to honor.

Something spill? Better wipe that up. There's dead plant matter in your grow tray or on the floor around your setup? Best clean that up and get rid of it. Infestations and infections love to grow in these conditions. So, check your plants, test the water, clean up the beds and show them a little love. You wouldn't let your dog sleep in its own waste, so why would you let your plants? Maintaining your garden is the most important thing you can do as a new grower.

Treat your plants right.

Mistake: Forgetting to Have Fun

HYDROPONICS

If you are growing because you want to sell your crops, that's a fine reason to do it. But try to have fun. For many, this is an enjoyable hobby and brings them a lot of peace. When you start to get money involved, it can be easy to lose track of that. Don't forget to take time to smell the roses. Or the tomatoes, whatever it is you're growing.

HYDROPONICS

Chapter Summary

- You want to design your hydroponic garden so that it is easy to get at all of your plants and access the reservoir without bumping into things or knocking over your lights.

- While many people who grow illegal crops use hydroponic gardens, there is nothing illegal about the systems of hydroponics nor does it need to be used for illegal means.

- Make sure you find out if the plants you want to grow will work for your climate.

- Indoor gardens offer us more control of our hydroponic environment but this does not mean that you have to put your hydroponic garden inside.

- Always do your research on the plants you want to grow. Make sure that they work in your setup, environment, and at your pH/EC levels.

- Hydroponics can be an expensive hobby but it doesn't cost a lot of money to get started and there are many DIY guides available to help you get into growing.

HYDROPONICS

- Start small and work your way up to a large garden so that you know how to best take care of your plants.

- There is nothing unnatural about hydroponic gardening.

- Remove dead plant matter, clean up spills, check the pH and EC levels. Not maintaining your garden is a sure-fire way to lose it and the biggest mistake new growers make.

- Have fun out there!

FINAL WORDS

We've come a long way throughout the course of this book. Starting with a definition of hydroponics, we're covered a lot of information that will help you to get started on your own hydroponic garden. Before we close, let's go over a brief summary of what we covered and share some words on where to go from here.

Hydroponics has been around for literally ages but it is only just starting to pick up some serious interest. These gardens can take a bit of work to set up and maintain but they offer a great way of growing crops. We focused here on those looking to get started with hydroponics, so we tailored our information towards the beginner. The lessons we covered, however, have everything the beginner needs to get started and begin the road to expert.

We have six primary setups to choose from when it comes to what kind of system we want to set up. We saw how to set up deep water, wicking and drip systems. These are the easiest systems for DIY setups and beginners but there are also aeroponics, ebb and flow and nutrient film technique systems. These systems are more complicated than is recommended for a beginner but I encourage you to research these more as you get more comfortable with hydroponics.

HYDROPONICS

There are four key elements that we looked at as the operation cycle of the hydroponic garden. These are soiling, seeding, lighting and trimming. By understanding how each of these elements works, we are able to handle the growing cycle of our plants. There are many options available for soiling and several for lighting. Finding the combination that is right for you will take some research but it should ultimately be decided on what plants you want to grow.

Speaking of plants, we have seen that there are a ton of plants that work really well in hydroponic gardens. Herbs grown in a hydroponic garden have 30% more aromatic oils than those grown in soil. Lettuce in particular absolutely adores growing hydroponically. Each plant has its own preferences when it comes to how much water it wants, the pH level it likes best and the temperature that it needs to grow. For this reason, we have to research our plants and make sure that we only grow those that are compatible together.

We also learned how to mix our own nutrient solutions so that we can provide our plants with what they need to grow. There are a lot of pre-mixed options available for purchase as well. Taking control of our own mix is just another way we are able to get closer to our plants and provide for them to the best of our ability.

The importance of maintaining a clean garden cannot be stressed enough and so we spent time learning

HYDROPONICS

how we care for our gardens. The information in chapter five can be used to build your own maintenance schedule. To do this, look at how often each step of maintenance needs to be performed and plan ahead so that you don't forget. It's super important that we take care of our plants because we don't want them in dirty environments nor do we want them to be overly stressed. A dirty environment and a stressed plant are a recipe for infestation and infection.

We explored some of the most common pests that attack our plants. However, we didn't cover all of them. That would take a whole book. The pests we covered are the most likely ones you will have to deal with but that doesn't mean they will be the only ones. It is a good thing we also learned how to prevent pests. The preventive steps we learned will also help us to spot any pests we did not cover. If you find something you don't recognize in one of your traps then you know it's time for more research. Remember too that not every insect is a pest, some help us out by eating pests!

Infection is a risk with all gardens and so our number one tool in preventing harmful pathogens from attacking our plants is to make sure that our plants are nice and strong. We clean our gardens, we provide them with nutrients mixed to their liking, we give them the love and care they need and in doing this we keep them healthy and unstressed. While infection can still take hold in a healthy plant, it is far more likely to attack stressed plants. This preventative step combines what we learned in chapter six about pests and infection with the skills we practice in chapter five.

Finally, we looked at mistakes that are common to beginning hydroponic gardeners. We also exploded those myths that surround hydroponics to dispel the lies and untruths surrounding our newfound hobby. Searching online for tips or mistakes will reveal many discussions with hydroponic gardeners that are written specifically to help beginners like you to have the easiest, most enjoyable time possible getting into this form of gardening.

If you're excited to get started then I suggest you begin planning out your garden now. You will need to dedicate a space for it and pick which system is most appealing to you and your skill level. Write down the plants you are most interested in growing and begin gathering information about them; what environment do they like best? What temperature? How much light do they need? What pH level?

Once you know what plants you want to grow and what system you want, you can start to build a shopping list. Along with the hardware to set up the system itself, don't forget to get some pH testing kits and an EC meter. Also make sure you have cleaning material, as you know now how important it is to sanitize and sterilize your equipment. This is also a great time to build your maintenance schedule.

Once you have this information you can return to this book and use it as a manual for walking through every step of the growing process. The information that we covered will take you from beginner and, along with the application of practice, turn you into a pro in no time. But most importantly, don't forget to have fun!

www.ingramcontent.com/pod-product-compliance
Lightning Source LLC
Chambersburg PA
CBHW050311120526
44592CB00014B/1862